THE **COMPLETE IDIOT'S GUIDE** TO

Being a New Dad

by Joe Kelly

ALPHA

A member of Penguin Group (USA) Inc.

For Mark Stelzner, New Dad

ALPHA BOOKS

Published by Penguin Group (USA) Inc.

Penguin Group (USA) Inc., 375 Hudson Street, New York, New York 10014, USA • Penguin Group (Canada), 90 Eglinton Avenue East, Suite 700, Toronto, Ontario M4P 2Y3, Canada (a division of Pearson Penguin Canada Inc.) • Penguin Books Ltd., 80 Strand, London WC2R 0RL, England • Penguin Ireland, 25 St. Stephen's Green, Dublin 2, Ireland (a division of Penguin Books Ltd.) • Penguin Group (Australia), 250 Camberwell Road, Camberwell, Victoria 3124, Australia (a division of Pearson Australia Group Pty. Ltd.) • Penguin Books India Pvt. Ltd., 11 Community Centre, Panchsheel Park, New Delhi—110 017, India • Penguin Group (NZ), 67 Apollo Drive, Rosedale, North Shore, Auckland 1311, New Zealand (a division of Pearson New Zealand Ltd.) • Penguin Books (South Africa) (Pty.) Ltd., 24 Sturdee Avenue, Rosebank, Johannesburg 2196, South Africa • Penguin Books Ltd., Registered Offices: 80 Strand, London WC2R 0RL, England

International Standard Book Number: 978-1-61564-2-472
Library of Congress Catalog Card Number: 2012951733

15   14   13   8   7   6   5   4   3   2   1

Interpretation of the printing code: The rightmost number of the first series of numbers is the year of the book's printing; the rightmost number of the second series of numbers is the number of the book's printing. For example, a printing code of 13-1 shows that the first printing occurred in 2013.

Printed in the United States of America

Note: This publication contains the opinions and ideas of its author. It is intended to provide helpful and informative material on the subject matter covered. It is sold with the understanding that the author and publisher are not engaged in rendering professional services in the book. If the reader requires personal assistance or advice, a competent professional should be consulted.

The author and publisher specifically disclaim any responsibility for any liability, loss, or risk, personal or otherwise, which is incurred as a consequence, directly or indirectly, of the use and application of any of the contents of this book.

Most Alpha books are available at special quantity discounts for bulk purchases for sales promotions, premiums, fund-raising, or educational use. Special books, or book excerpts, can also be created to fit specific needs. For details, write: Special Markets, Alpha Books, 375 Hudson Street, New York, NY 10014.

Publisher: *Mike Sanders*
Executive Managing Editor: *Billy Fields*
Acquisitions Editor: *Brook Farling*
Development Editor: *Jennifer Moore*
Senior Production Editor: *Janette Lynn*
Copy Editor: *Daron Thayer*

Cover Designer: *Rebecca Batchelor*
Book Designers: *William Thomas, Rebecca Batchelor*
Indexer: *Tonya Heard*
Layout: *Ayanna Lacey*
Proofreader: *Tricia Liebig*

Contents

Part 1:   **Spring Training** 1

   1   **What Did I Get Myself Into?** 3

       Freaked Out? 3

           Are You Crazy? 4

           Anybody Seen the Manual? 6

       You Will Screw Up—and Survive 7

           Honoring Mistakes 7

           Who's the Expert? 8

       A Dose of Daddy Data 9

           Even Your B.O. Helps 9

           Better Than Broccoli 11

           Good for Her and Us, Too 12

       Your Own Kind of Dad 13

           Can My Parents Be Salvaged? 13

           Child to Dad 15

           Not Married? Still Dad 16

       You Have What It Takes 17

           Nature Provides 18

           The Expert Next Door 19

   2   **Preparing the Field** 21

       Making a Nursery 21

           Thinking It Through 22

           Choosing the Spot 23

           Design and Layout 24

           Check the Clock 25

       Sleeping Beauty 26

           Cradles 26

           Cribs 27

           Crib Assembly 28

           Crib Bling 29

       The Rest of the Gear 30

           Changing Table 31

           Diapering Decisions 32

           Rocking Chair 33

           Infant Seat and High Chair 34

           Nursery Supplies 35

           Bath Gear 36

Childproofing the House 37
    Smoke Alarm 37
    The Kitchen 38
    Living Areas 39

3   Away Games 41
Buyer Beware 41
Car Seat 42
    Why Use One? 43
    How to Use One 44
    Combo, Cash, and Convenience 45
Strollers 46
Play Pens, a.k.a. Play Yards 48
Carrying Contraptions... 49
Climate Considerations... 50
    Hot Times.. 50
    Cold Calls 51

4   Drafting Personnel...53
OBs, Midwives, and Other Aliens 53
    Making Your Pick...55
    Enough Tests—This Is No Peepshow! 57
    Your First Visit 58
    Pink, Blue, Up to You 59
    Do I Have to Watch the Bloody Birth? 59
Finding the Right Pediatrician 61
Choosing Child Care 62
    Using a Pro 62
    Bringing It Home 63
    At-Home Moms and Dads.. 64
Family and Friends 65
Psst. Mom, Over Here... 66
    The Invisible Gatekeeper.. 66
    Sharing the Load... 67

5   Exhibition Games...69
The Great Mimic... 69
D'ya Hear About the Baby with Four Ears? 70
One Last R&R 71

Coaching the Quarterback..72

    Coaching Styles.. 72

    The Gameday Playsheet 74

I Have Needs, Too, Ya Know 75

    Real Men Don't Get Stressed................................76

    Ignore the Score 77

    I Don't Need a Doctor to Be Healthy.................... 78

    Garbage In, Garbage Out................................... 79

Extreme Makeover: Home Edition 81

Part 2: Opening Day 83

6 Ready, Set, Go! 85

Birthday Plans...85

    Pre-Flight Screening.. 86

    Birthday Bag for Three, Please 87

Signs of the Time 90

    "False" Labor..91

    Now Appearing on Stage One 91

    Hit the Road, Jack 94

Hospital Hijinks.. 94

    Phase Two..95

    Phase Three 96

You're No Bench Player... 96

7 Can I Survive This Birth?..............................99

What to Say and Stifle... 99

Labor 1.2 and Its Upgrade, 1.3 101

    What to Do in Phase Two 101

    Phase Three to Delivery.....................................102

Make Way for Baby 103

    Elastic Momma, Queasy Poppa..........................103

    How Much Pain Is Too Much Pain? 104

    Dumping the Drug Debate.................................105

Slow Poke Moms 106

Stage Two and What to Do 107

    Push 'em Out, Shove 'em Out! 107

    Your Delivery Party 107

The Crowning Moment 108
    Episiotomy *109*
    Where's Daddy? *109*
    Umbilical Options *111*
    Apgar and Co. *112*
    We're Not Done Yet! Stage Three *113*
A Change in Plans 113
    Caesarean Sections *114*
    Dad's Caesarean Role *115*
    Breech Birth *116*
Don't Try This at Home, If You Can Help It 117
Tweet or Consequences 118

8   Father's Day Is Here 121
Babies Don't Break 121
    Call Me Unpredictable *122*
    Holding the Baby *123*
The Kid's First First Aid Kit 125
If Daddy Could Breastfeed 126
    Dad-Baby Bottlenecks *126*
    Her Breasts Work Fine for Me! *127*
    Bottled Magic *129*
    Burping and Spitting Up—Yum! *129*
Changing a Diaper 131
Diaper Rash 132
Caring for Mom 133
    The Blue and the Grey *134*
    Baby on Parade *134*
    Me Time, Us Time *135*
I'm So Frustrated, I Could Scream 137
Go, Baby! 138

**9   Scoring: Sex (and Other Relations) for
New Dads 141**
Lessons in Practical Physics: Sex During Pregnancy 142
    Moaning Over Hormones *142*
    You'll Poke the Baby's Eye Out (Not) *144*
    Ballooning *145*
    Sex and the Bump *146*

Keep Your Eyes Offa Her! 147

Sex After Childbirth: The Next Frontier 148

Is Snoring Sexy? *149*

Back in Play *150*

While You Wait *151*

Sharing Her Breasts *152*

Fishing for Romance *153*

Part 3: The First Season **155**

10 Finding the Sweet Spot **157**

ET, Phone ER 157

Bonding Is Ensured 158

Routine Rotations 159

It Worked for Me! *160*

Shhhhh! Baby's in the House *161*

Knowing the Score *162*

When to Call the Doctor 164

Disciples of Discipline 165

Infant Morality *165*

Loving's the Limit *167*

Playing Games 169

Dad: No Batteries Needed *170*

Toy Talk *171*

11 Game Changers: Nontraditional Fatherhood **175**

ESP and Co-Parenting 176

Creating a Parenting Plan 177

Gay Dads 178

Teen Dads 179

Middle-Age Dads 181

Live-Away Dads 182

Insuring Your Baby 184

Tackling Touch Taboos 186

Identifying Good Touch *187*

Plugging In to Tune In *187*

12 Off and Running: Months Two to Six **189**

Heads Up! Month Two 189

You in Two 190

Sleeptime Strategies That (Might) Work 192

Resent-o-Rama 194

This Is Personal: Month Three 194

Your First Talk 195

Bath or Water Fight? 196

Does He Like Me Best? Month Four 197

You Call This Solid Food? 198

Still Talking Nonsense 199

Orally Fixated: Month Five 199

Your Moving Target 200

In the Swing 200

So, That's Why We Named Him: Month Six 201

Uncovering Your Skill Sets 202

13 Taking a Walk: Months Seven to Twelve **203**

Perpetual Motion: Month Seven 204

Your Reentry Orbit 204

Jealous or Jolly? 205

It's a Kid! Month Eight 205

You Be the Judge 206

Staying on Radar 207

Standing Fine in Month Nine 208

Sign Up 208

His Teeth Are Killing Me 209

Your Baby's EMT 210

Speed Demon: Month Ten 211

The World's Strongest Two-Letter Word 211

Valuable Veterans 212

Walking Wonders: Month 11 212

Stir and Chill 213

Index **215**

Introduction

Who knew that pregnancy, labor, and delivery could be such a wild ride? What blockbuster thriller has such wild mood swings—from excitement to terror and back to euphoria?

And that's all before you even take your baby home from the hospital.

Your child's first year is the most intense of her life. That year (and the months before she's born) are likely to be one of the most intense—and wonderful—years of your life, too.

You're now a father, the highest honor a man can hold. As with any honor, there is glory and uncertainty. You will burst with pride, and you'll wonder how you suddenly got the capacity to love someone this much. You won't have all of the answers, and you'll wonder how you'll afford all that's ahead. At least you can take some comfort from all the dads who've gone before you.

You are not alone. Through the centuries, millions of other fathers also swelled with pride and recoiled from uncertainty. Yet, somehow, the human species keeps surviving and thriving through the good— if imperfect—parenting of fathers and mothers. Guys keep getting in the game because, as one veteran dad says, "Fatherhood is the greatest experience known to man."

Most fathers through history did their jobs without ever reading a book. That long, natural heritage lays a pretty solid foundation for you. Still, despite the millennia of fathering experience, it takes conscious effort (and sometimes even a bit of pushiness) for a man to stay involved in child-rearing nowadays.

So why bother with a book? If you're like most men, your own father probably didn't give you tons of instruction on how to be a dad (because he probably didn't get any from your grandpa). Most men lack a surefire road map for making the Peter Parker-like transformation from ordinary guy to something stronger and more agile than Spiderman—DAD.

This book gives you that map. *The Complete Idiot's Guide to Being a New Dad* combines fathering "wisdom of the ages" with new insights to guide you through your first year as Daddy.

I am a father; my twin daughters survived my parenting and are in their 30s. I've worked in the parenting field for many years and have been lucky enough to talk to thousands of fathers, and this book draws on their experiences, too.

So, as you step off the pregnancy ride and enter the roller coaster of fatherhood, keep this "game plan" nearby to help you survive and enjoy this first year of the ride of your life.

This book will show you:

- Why and how to avoid being left behind in the merry-go-round of doctors' visits, diaper changes, opinionated relatives, teething, and the other challenges of your child's first year.

- How to use your provider and protector instincts to help create healthy, enjoyable child-rearing for you, your partner, and your baby (or babies).

- How to make room in your home, finances, career, and psyche for your baby.

- How to share this miracle with your partner (and your baby) as fully as possible.

When you're done with the book, you won't be a Superhero Dad with a magic fathering cape. But you will have much of the equipment for the most exciting job you'll ever have, and you'll know how to keep your balance.

Best of all, you'll learn how much you already knew about being a dad, and how that knowledge can give you confidence in your fathering abilities for decades to come. (Yes, I said decades; once a dad, always a dad.)

Welcome to the brotherhood of Fathers!

Just a couple of notes about words. Sometimes I think the term "partner" perfectly describes the rich, complicated, shared, spiritual nature of the 34 years I've spent (so far) with my wife, Nancy. Other times, it sounds like a cold description of someone in a shady law firm. But, I use "partner" in the book anyway, because many dads aren't married to the mothers of their children, and some children are raised by two dads. Bottom line: "partner" is an imperfect word—and, like good partners, let's shake on it and move on.

Some babies are boys and some are girls. (This really is an Idiot's Guide!) So, because no child is an "it," I sometimes call the baby she, and other times he.

How This Book Is Organized

I've divided the book into three parts.

Part 1, Spring Training, tackles what you need to do over the final weeks before your baby is born. That includes getting your home ready to be safe for baby and efficient for Dad and Mom. I give you tips for picking the players to help your child grow up healthy. You may not get everything done ahead of time, but at least you'll have a comprehensive and clear list. Then, I offer some guidance for surviving those intense last days before baby comes.

Part 2, Opening Day, starts with your child's birth day and covers all the ins and outs—especially the "out comes baby" details. You get solid instructions on holding, feeding, diapering, burping, and calming your newborn. I give you tips on making the transition from hospital to home and help you manage relatives, visitors, and unsolicited advice. You also get help with a solid co-parenting plan with your partner.

Part 3, The First Season, shows you the way from infancy to toddlerhood. It also has straight talk about rediscovering your sexual and intimate rhythm after childbirth. You learn basics about adjusting to baby's rapid growth and changes, discipline, work-family balance, and keeping yourself in the game. You also get the scoop on baby's development, making mistakes, and that pressing global question: Is fatherhood better than sex?

Extras

Look for these handy sidebars throughout the book—they have important concepts you need to get the most out of your amazing first months of fatherhood.

DAD WORDS

Humorous, inspirational, and/or instructive quotes from celebrities, authors, and veteran dads. The names of the less famous were changed for their own protection.

EXTRA POINT

Simple (and sometimes counterintuitive) tips on practical child-rearing skills, like calming a baby, changing diapers, going to the doctor, and otherwise getting through the day.

HEADS UP

Warnings about common dangers, missteps, and misconceptions in the new baby game.

READING THE SIGNS

Tips for tuning in to your partner, your baby, and you as you build deep, lifelong family bonds.

Acknowledgments

Thanks to Bill Klatte, Armin Brott, Will Glennon, Michael Kimmel, and John Badalament for their guidance and work on fathering and manhood; R. Clarence Jones, Joy Dorscher, MD, Amy Chezem, Sam Simmons, Melissa Froehle, Paul Masiarchin, and Judge David Peterson for their expert guidance; and to the thousands of men who've shared their stories with me over the years. For help in birthing the book, my thanks to Brook Farling, Marilyn Allen,

Coleen O'Shea, Ryan Ruffcorn, Steve Knauss, Dusty Johnson, the late Kevin Karr, John Parker and Naomi Saks, Petra Liljestrand and Alice Phillipson, Mike Sanders, and the Starbucks crews in Oakland and Emeryville, California. Special thanks to Mark Stelzner, who is reintroducing me to the experiences of an expectant father (and helping make me a grandfather) and Maya Phillipson, the world's best aunt. Most of all, thanks to Nancy Gruver, Nia Kelly, and Mavis Gruver, the gals who made me a dad.

Trademarks

All terms mentioned in this book that are known to be or are suspected of being trademarks or service marks have been appropriately capitalized. Alpha Books and Penguin Group (USA) Inc. cannot attest to the accuracy of this information. Use of a term in this book should not be regarded as affecting the validity of any trademark or service mark.

Spring Training

Welcome to your new life. You're new to the roster of a team—fathers—that can't put you on waivers. You'll play forever without retiring or being cut.

Meanwhile, you have to get through pregnancy and childbirth. That should be easy, because pregnancy and childbirth happen to the mother, right? Well, not so much.

In this part of the book, you explore how much your life changes even before your baby arrives, and how pregnancy hints at the demands of raising an infant. You find out how much your healthy and active involvement benefits your baby, your partner, you, and your marriage or relationship.

You get practical tips on preparing your home (and budget) for a newborn, how to pick a doctor, come up with a birth plan, and take other steps to prepare you and your partner for your baby's big birth day.

Most important, you'll learn how much you have to contribute, how much you know without knowing it, and that you *will* survive!

What Did I Get Myself Into?

In This Chapter

- Keeping the panic at bay
- Avoiding the parent trap
- Following your instincts
- Asking for help and advice

You're a father. Simple sentence, right? Simple concept? Not so much. Welcome to a state of simultaneous excitement, dread, enthusiasm, panic, pride, and confusion … fatherhood!

Once you are a dad, you can never be "not-a-dad" anymore. By becoming a father, you embark on an amazing, profound, powerful, and fulfilling journey that starts even before the moment of birth.

This chapter gives you some hints on how to think about your fathering style, so you can get from delivery or adoption day to the day your child says adios to you and your home. There is no turning back now (hospitals and adoption agencies don't do exchanges or refunds!), so let's leap in to this amazing journey together.

Freaked Out?

Here are three things you need to know about fathering:

- It's like a roller coaster.
- You can't know for sure how your actions will affect your child.
- You can guarantee that your actions do affect your child.

So, if your first reaction is panic, it's not a big deal. Really! Almost every father freezes when thinking about the enormous responsibility of being a dad. In fact, you may have more fatherly panic attacks over the next 18, 21, or even 50 years, so get used to them.

But it's also going to be a blast—get used to having a lot of great times, too!

HEADS UP

Don't believe the myth that fathers aren't important to their kids. You matter a lot—and you have what it takes to be a good dad.

Most of us grew up learning that a father's biggest responsibilities are to provide and protect. As soon as you know that you're expecting or are a new dad, you feel a lot more protective of your partner and baby, both physically and psychologically. You naturally wonder whether you can be a good enough provider.

Fortunately, you don't need lots of money to be a good provider. Sure, you need money and resources to take proper care of your child, but she needs your time and attention even more—at least until she's a teenager (when she'll think she needs just the money, but she'll be wrong).

Are You Crazy?

If you're like most new or soon-to-be new dads, you have questions that are hard to talk about with anyone else. Over the course of this book, I tackle such questions honestly, practically, and with a few laughs.

Some of your questions are practical:

- Do I have or make enough money to afford a family?
- Will I break the baby?
- Will I get sick and pass out in the delivery room?

Some questions are deeply personal:

- Can I share my partner with someone else—even a baby?
- Will I love (or even like) my child?
- Will I know how to raise a child?

Other questions may be a bit scary:

- Do I really want to go through with this?
- Does this mean I can't have fun anymore?
- What if she grows up to be a teenager who spends time around boys like I was at that age?

Of course, you might even wonder whether you're crazy or weird even to have these kinds of questions.

Don't worry; there's nothing wrong with you. You're normal. Nearly every father asks at least one of these questions, and many others, too.

Which is actually good news! You're not alone; for millennia, men have felt ecstatic and panicked when they hear those magic words: "You're gonna be a dad!"

So why do we panic? Because no one has ever been so completely dependent on us as this baby will be. It feels wonderful to be so needed, but it's also a bit scary. Fortunately, you have more fathering resources at your disposal than you may think.

Your protector and provider instincts will be very handy over the coming months and the next couple of decades (no way around it, most kids stick around at least that long). Used wisely, those instincts can do more than you (or anyone else) thought possible to make parenting the healthiest and most enjoyable experience possible for you, your partner, and your new child.

Plus, along with the panic, you'll also start feeling great pride in your accomplishment. Rightly so! Pride will continue to be a great comfort and motivation through all your days as a father.

Anybody Seen the Manual?

Ever heard someone say, "Men never read the instructions?" Nonsense.

True, we might skip the instructions (temporarily!) because it's challenging and fun trying with our wits alone to assemble a model airplane, build a computer, or master Level XXIII of a video game.

We're good at learning things on our own—and using tools to improve our skills. Take the complex and apparently infinite functions of Photoshop. We'll fool around with it out of the box, eventually read the manual, get *The Complete Idiot's Guide* to the latest version, and use the hundreds of YouTube tutorials to make the most of the program's power.

You can make a strong case that raising kids is more important than tweaking photographs, so of course there's an owner's manual for your new child, right? Well … there is one little glitch.

There is no owner's manual for your child. Although she is a mobile version (with a very active "squirm" function), she has no plug-and-play attachments or downloadable upgrades. There isn't even an app. There is no set-in-stone formula for the pregnancy, your child's life from infancy to adulthood, or your life from her infancy to adulthood.

There's not even a government authority to give you new father training, tests, and a license—like the DMV did when you learned to drive for the first time.

In the movie *Parenthood*, the teen dad Tod (played by Keanu Reeves) says, "You need a license to buy a dog or drive a car. Hell, you even need a license to catch a fish. But they'll let any [expletive deleted] a**hole be a father."

With that bit of earthy humor, Tod explains the biggest dilemma a new father faces: No one trained me for this job.

If you're reading this book, being a horrible dad is clearly not your goal. You want to be a good and competent father. That's very good news for you, your partner, and your kid. So, is there any way to get the information and guidance that nonexistent, good-for-all-makes-and-models owner's manual would provide?

Information and guidance, yes. But it's much harder to find surefire answers that will always work for you and your child. But not to worry!

You Will Screw Up—and Survive

By the power invested in me by the publisher of *Complete Idiot's Guides*, I hereby grant you permission to make mistakes as a father.

None of us want to make mistakes, damage our children, or hurt the people we love. Doing the right thing is our fatherly obligation—and opportunity. But as you know from your own life, good intentions don't always prevent screw-ups.

> **EXTRA POINT**
>
> Too many parents today think that their job is to remove all the bumps in the road of their child's life. That's impossible. A more important job is to equip your children with good shock absorbers so they learn to handle the bumps themselves.
>
> —David Walsh, PhD

Nobody wants to see their children get hurt. You will suffer when you see your kid fall down (although that may happen to you less often than to mom). You will want to hover and/or rush in to rescue him from trouble. That's not always the best strategy, as you'll soon see when your child starts learning to walk. He will fall repeatedly, bang into things, get bruises, scream loudly—and then laugh loudly and proudly when all those falls teach him to walk on his own.

Honoring Mistakes

As you attempt to father well, you're going to make mistakes, some of which will seem pretty dumb. Let's face it, some actually will be dumb. But you can't let your mistakes stop you, any more than your infant will let his "mistake" of falling down keep him from learning to walk.

After decades of talking with fathers and stepfathers, I'm convinced that mistakes are very valuable. Stop and think about some of the important life lessons you learned over the years. Now think about when, where, how, and why you earned those bits of wisdom. Chances are good that you learned some (if not most) of these lessons in the process (or aftermath) of a major screw-up.

Of course, you will learn important aspects of good fathering from your successes. (Honey, guess what? Singing Lady Gaga's "Poker Face" got the baby to sleep every night this week!) And you'll learn from trial and error, too. Both ways are okay!

It can be tempting to beat yourself up for a mistake, and some people may say you're making a mistake just because you're doing things differently than your mom did (more on that later). But getting down on yourself doesn't help you, your baby, or your family.

Think of mistakes as a bonus chance to learn. Getting in that habit can teach your child a lot as he gets older, too. Not to mention how much easier it'll be to accept your child's mistakes (say, in 13 to 20 years from now), and see them as opportunities for him to learn life lessons that experience alone can teach.

Who's the Expert?

Depending on how you look at it, the lack of foolproof fathering instructions can be liberating. Pioneering pediatric psychologist Lee Salk (brother of Jonas, creator of the polio vaccine) urged parents to trust their natural connection to their children. As a new dad, I took comfort and confidence from his advice.

In a refreshing departure for a parenting author, Salk argued that we shouldn't worry so much about what the latest parenting book says. His book *What Every Child Would Like His Parents to Know* wisely encouraged me to trust my heart along with my baby's sounds and body. If I "tuned in" to my deep fathering instincts, and the signals my infants "broadcast," I'd have most of what I'd need to be a good father. As fathering expert Will Glennon says, "The key is to father from the heart."

That's not to say that the many resources available to new fathers today are useless. (Let's hope not! Otherwise, who else will buy this book?)

DAD WORDS

I never had a speech from my father "this is what you must do or shouldn't do" but I just learned to be led by example. My father wasn't perfect.

—Adam Sandler

But keep in mind the two best things any "new parent" resource can do:

- Give you some sturdy bricks for your fathering foundation and flexible panes of glass for the walls.
- Encourage you to build your own unique greenhouse in which to raise a vibrant, lush, and well-rooted child.

The point is that you can and will create your own way of fathering while also sharing hundreds of common experiences with your fellow fathers. So, use "expert" parenting resources as guides, not commands from on high.

A Dose of Daddy Data

Social science researchers are famous (or infamous) for their lack of unanimity on any aspect of human relations. It's a lot like politics; people can find all sorts of reasons to support a position—or its exact opposite. You know Harry Truman's famous line: "There are three kinds of lies: Lies, damned lies, and statistics."? (Truman also spoke about his father, whose farm and grain trading business collapsed in the early 1900s: "My father was not a failure; after all, he was the father of a president of the United States.")

Now, back to the statistics. One of the few things almost all psychological and social research agrees on is this: Children benefit a lot when loving and informed fathers and/or stepfathers are actively involved in their lives.

Even Your B.O. Helps

Psychiatrist Kyle Pruett, MD, a professor at the Yale University Child Study Center, says a father's importance starts with his very presence: "[H]is smells, textures, voice, rhythms, [and] size promote an awareness in his child that it is okay to be different and okay to desire and love the inherently different, the not-mother entities of the world."

The odds that a child will grow up healthier and more resilient improve when dad is integral to her upbringing. If a dad actively raises his child during her first six months, she will achieve higher development in several areas. Social science research suggests that a kid with an actively involved father is likely to benefit intellectually, so that she will ...

- Learn to read sooner and better.
- Develop a higher preschool IQ.
- For girls, have higher preschool math competence and be more willing to try new things.
- Graduate high school and attend college.

Highly involved dads also help their children develop physically to ...

- Be more comfortable with physicality and physical risk.
- If female, reach puberty at a later age.
- Be better at problem-solving.

And, to top it off, good father involvement helps kids develop socially so they ...

- Have a stronger sense of humor.
- Cope better with stress and frustration.
- Act out less.
- Be more comfortable with and accepting of people who disagree with her.

Several studies indicate that when their fathers read to their children, the kids develop higher verbal skills than when their mothers alone read to them. Particularly during the first year of life, avid father participation in child-rearing strengthens the infant's cognitive function.

DAD WORDS

My father had a profound influence on me. He was a lunatic.

—Spike Milligan (creator of "The Goon Show")

I'm not saying that every child who grows up without close ties to her father (due to death, divorce, illness, incarceration, and so on) is doomed to a dreary life of endless failure. That's nonsense. We can all find people who grew up without a caring father—or any father at all. They may face certain struggles (like people who grow up without mothers), but they're still capable of becoming competent adults with success and friends.

Of course, father care is not the only factor that gives kids an edge. But it does matter—and it has other great side effects!

Better Than Broccoli

Believe it or not, even with all of fathering's demands and the steep learning curve, actively involved dads are healthier and happier than the average man. Yes, fathering is very good for you, and (at least in my book) it's a lot more fun than the nutritional strategies of Popeye (eating spinach out of a can) or my wife (eating broccoli). Not that you shouldn't eat vegetables (they're allegedly good for you), but both spinach and fathering are better when they don't come in cans.

According to fathering researchers, involved fathers are more likely to be productive and responsible at work, take fewer sick days, and move up the career ranks. Fathers who continue to learn and get better at managing the demands of child-rearing tend to do better managing other life demands and feel good about themselves as a result.

Ask a veteran father if he's learned anything from his children, and he will almost surely say, "Of course!" From day one, our children teach us amazing things about the world, our families, themselves, and ourselves. Now that this individual child has entered your life, the two of you will reveal miraculous new things about yourselves to each other on a regular (if not daily) basis.

Veteran dads will also tell you that the more you nurture your child, the more you will feel nurtured by him in return. This is only one of many paradoxes of parenting. Especially in the first year, you will crave the times that your baby responds to you because it makes you feel euphoric and deeply content.

Good for Her and Us, Too

You and your baby are not the only beneficiaries of your active fathering. Statistically, the mother of your child is more likely to be happier and healthier. And to top it off, the relationship between mom and dad tends to be happier and healthier when dad shares the parenting equally.

Mothers have told pollsters for years that their biggest stress is managing all the demands of child-rearing, even if they don't also have the demands of a paying job (which most moms do have). So, the more parenting responsibilities a father takes on, the greater the chance that his partner's stress level will drop, making her a happier camper.

Not only that, some research indicates that mothers are better at their mothering when fathers share the everyday parenting. These moms show more patience, emotional openness, and flexibility toward their children—and their partners (this means you!).

That makes sense, because a new child generally happens to two people. The more those two adults share the responsibility (and opportunity), the more likely that the job gets done well.

It also stands to reason that reducing stress for one partner in a relationship reduces stress in the relationship itself. That opens the door for more happiness in the relationship, and for the two people in it. There might be some chicken-and-egg forces at work here, too, because men who are happy in their marriage are more likely to be actively involved fathers, and reinforce the whole circle of good stuff that comes from making that commitment.

To top it off, some research indicates that siblings interact with each other better when their father is active in child-rearing, which means your involvement may make your entire family a better place to live and grow up.

Despite all the benefits of active fathering, there can be many barriers to that involvement, which we'll discuss throughout the book. That's why it's so important for you to consciously advocate for your involvement every day.

Your Own Kind of Dad

Believe it or not, despite all this data, some people (including men) continue to ask whether fathers matter all that much to children. Well, stop and ask yourself how your relationship (or lack thereof) with your father or stepfather affected your life. Ask almost anyone else you know the same question.

The answers you get will make a compelling case for the impact of dads.

Let me be clear, fathers are not more important than mothers. Nor are fathers less important than mothers. It's not a matter of keeping score about who is better or more necessary—keeping score accomplishes squat in raising kids. Mothers and fathers are similar in many ways and different in some interesting and important ways.

But the way you father doesn't have to be dictated by stale, outdated notions of "what fathers do and what mothers do."

The bottom line is simple: a child needs committed, involved parents and stepparents.

Your experience and your qualities as a person mean more to your child than your gender does. You can be your own kind of dad from the start, creating your unique, fun, and wonderful relationship with your child. You can do it!

Can My Parents Be Salvaged?

If you're lucky, your parents and stepparents may seem like a mother lode (why aren't there father lodes?) of good ways to parent. Meanwhile, some of our parents seem more like a junk heap of bad examples ripe for plowing under as soon as possible.

For most of us, though, our parents are a nice, earthy mix of good and bad.

As a new father, this could be a good time to take an honest, detached look at how your parents, stepparents, grandparents, and other adults raised you (and your sibs and step-sibs). Even if that view shows only a massive mound of manure, there is still probably something in there to salvage.

As my grandmother used to say, "Even a stopped clock is right twice a day." (Of course, that saying made more sense back before digital clocks, but you get the idea.)

Remember that the same parental behavior can feel great or terrible, depending on the circumstances. Your dad's hugs may have been the most comforting thing in the world some days, and felt smothering on others. One day, his high expectations made you feel proud under the spotlight of his attention. Another day, it felt like rejection of who you were. Being a father is a complicated thing. So is being a child.

Becoming a father will probably change the way you feel about your stepparents and parents. As Oscar Wilde wrote: "Children begin by loving their parents. After a time they judge them. Rarely, if ever, do they forgive them." As a dad, you actually may feel more forgiving and appreciative of your parental units, or maybe less. Either way, there's a lot you can learn from them.

 DAD WORDS

Skate to where the puck is going, not where it's been.
—Wayne Gretzky

The key is taking a detached look at how they parented. You can do this before your baby is born, since you are not yet swept away by the distractions and intense emotions of parenting your own crying, giggling, walking, sassing, and adorable child. But afterward is valuable, too. As your own kind of father, you may see things in a different light now—including how you were raised.

Child to Dad

Because we grow up in it, we tend to accept our family's behavior as normal. I mean, you can't expect an 8-year-old to conduct sociological fieldwork in order to determine what's "normal" in families. But whatever its own "norm," our families have lots to teach us.

We have a shared heritage with our relatives and ancestors, which can provide a lot of background and support for our fathering. For example, I was raised Irish Catholic, with grandparents, aunts, uncles, and 14 first cousins living nearby. I also had many friends who were part of large families, so I learned to enjoy the hubbub of intense talk, loud laughter, and lots of little kids underfoot.

Looking back, I can see how that heritage worked its way unconsciously into my fathering. It was important for my kids and me to spend family time together (especially in the kitchen—did I mention that we're Irish?), and visit relatives often, just like my family did when I was young. I've remained close friends with cousins, who continue to teach me a lot about being good fathers. For example, my cousin Frank is one of the best divorced dads I know!

Family heritage (good or bad) comes to us through many channels. Distant and nearby relatives can share stories and examples for us. You can use this information to decide what elements of your heritage to embrace and what parts (if any) to reject. Thinking this through helps you create the heritage you want for your new child.

It's often hard to decipher how our own parents' and stepparents' influence our heritage. When something is very close to your eyes, it's hard to see where it fits into a larger picture and context.

Of course, our relationships with our parents and stepparents tend to be a bit more complicated, since they are the adults we were closest to growing up.

Now is a good time to seek perspective on the people who raised you and your partner. Remember that parenting is more art than science, no matter who is doing it. Nobody is or can be perfect (not you, your partner, your parents, your stepparents, your in-laws, or your child). Every one of your parents taught you at least one important lesson, even if it was the painful lesson of what not to do as a parent yourself.

HEADS UP

If you or your partner were (or suspect you were) abused as children, you can break the cycle. You were not at fault, and you *can* raise strong and healthy kids. See parentsanonymous.org and childhelp.org for online resources—and actively seek counseling to create a safer, better life for your new family.

Not Married? Still Dad

If you have a child outside of marriage, you will surely run into people (including relatives) who are less than pleased about you becoming a dad now. They will include people who think marriage should always come before pregnancy (and sex!), or people who think it is wrong for gay couples or single people to give birth or adopt.

Keep this in mind: Your commitment to your child and your partner are far more important than a relative's disapproving comments. Don't let people's opinions derail you from staying on track to being deeply involved in your child's life.

Be open, honest, accepting, and roll with the punches, even when they hurt. This is a skill, after all, that you'll need to practice more and more as the kid gets older and throws some of her own punches your way!

DAD WORDS

Most American children suffer from too much mother and too little father.

—Gloria Steinem

For example, I adored my grandfather and always craved his approval, so it hurt when he told me how disappointed he was that Nancy and I got pregnant before we got married.

Lucky for me, my grandfather was a wise man who didn't belabor the point (since he knew that wouldn't stop the birth) and he didn't stop showing his love. He only lived a few years longer, but said that one of the happiest days of his life was meeting our twins. He joyfully sat his creaky, 80-something body down on the floor so he could gurgle, chatter, and laugh with his first great-grandchildren.

His delight that day erased any hurt and anxiety I'd felt. After all, a happy great-grandfather was far more important for my kids than whether my feelings were bruised a few months beforehand.

Sure, a relative's reaction may hurt for a short time. But if everyone acts like adults, then the hurt will soon be forgotten in the excitement of your beautiful baby.

If some people choose not to act like adults, well, there's nothing you can do to change them, so don't try. You're far better off putting that energy into raising your kid well, so that when she becomes an adult, she'll act like one.

You Have What It Takes

The day you bring your newborn home with you is exciting and overwhelming. It's a cliché, but your life will never be the same. Your child is different from other children (heck, my identical twins came 14 minutes apart, yet they are markedly different from one other—as is my relationship with each of them). Your child is also different from you and your partner, even though you combined to make or adopt her. You and your partner are different than you were before, in ways you may not always be able to describe.

That's why each father-child bond is unique and continually evolving.

Amid all the mystery and excitement, you also need to know that you can do this fathering thing very well. The more you put into it, the better you'll do—and the more fun and satisfaction you will have.

This is true, even though few men learn much about taking care of kids when they are boys. Families with small children are still far more likely to hire a teenage girl for babysitting than a teenage boy. If you have younger siblings, worked at a summer camp, or coach a youth sport, then you know something about small children's ways.

But even if you have no experience with kids, you're not up a creek.

Nature Provides

For as long as humans have been around, fathers found ways of figuring things out. That's still true today.

For example, dads today have more freedom than ever to take "non-traditional" approaches to fathering. Many men take time away from their careers to stay home with the baby while their partners return to the workplace. Other men work part-time or telecommute so they can commune with baby every possible moment. Some men even teach Head Start and early childhood parent education classes!

You don't have to father the same way your father or grandfather did. If you want or need to, you can set your own pattern. That opportunity is liberating and exciting but can also be disconcerting. After all, it's harder to find role models when you're blazing a new path.

But we can usually rely on our fatherly instincts. For millennia, nature has made us essential in conceiving, birthing, and rearing children. There's plenty of good, useful heritage in our manly history and our genes. After all, your seminal participation produced this new child, so you will connect to her naturally.

If you're adopting, nature provides for you, too. Throughout history, adults have adopted and/or helped raise orphans, relatives, and neighbor children—building bonds as vibrant as any biological link. The more time and attention you give to your new child, the more you will know her, the closer you will become, and the more you will instinctively know the right things to do.

So, trust your gut; it's Nature's way of talking to you.

Nature provides other tools that you may not yet know about. For example, from the moment of birth, you and your baby can instinctively communicate with each other, even though it'll be a year or more before she uses words.

Your partner is another essential resource for you. You're raising this child together, even if you don't all live together. Share the experience, be willing to learn from your partner, and communicate, communicate, communicate. You have twice as many ears as mouths, so listen more than you talk.

The same thing goes for family members and friends whose parenting wisdom and experience you trust. Believe it or not, other parents are fonts of wisdom willing—even eager—to share their knowledge. Talk (and listen) to them, especially the dads.

The Expert Next Door

Billions of fathers, with billions of years of experience, walked the dad path before you. Fortunately, quite a few of them are still alive and kicking. Don't let them go to waste.

Think of those fathers and stepfathers (including your own) as resources, available to help you with research and questions. In a very real sense, these veteran fathers are walking encyclopedias of information, skill, experience, and lessons learned.

It is kind of silly not to take advantage of all that knowledge and wisdom. Still, fathers don't make a habit of talking to each other about being dads. We're more comfortable discussing the latest football trade than the pros and cons of going to infant swim classes at the Y.

Fortunately, you don't have to repeat any "strong and silent" or "fathering is for wimps" patterns. (Parenting is most definitely not for wimps.) So use your courage to ask an experienced father for advice. Or just ask him to tell stories about when he and his partner were first starting out. He'll probably be flattered, and happy to chat.

Find three or four neighbors or co-workers who are fathers and/or stepfathers. Ask them how old their children are, and then add up the ages of all their respective children to see how much fathering experience they have (for example, I have two 32-year-olds, so my total would be 64—even though I'm only 58). The odds are good that those three or four dads have accumulated close to a century of fathering know-how between them. It might be tough to come up with a situation that one of them hasn't encountered.

So, on the days when you feel panicked and overwhelmed, stop and ask for help and directions from a veteran dad or a parents' hotline or "warmline." Notice, I said "when" and not "if." You will feel panicked and overwhelmed, so don't … well, panic about it!

People around you are interested in helping you through your new adventure. Enjoy the conversations.

The Least You Need to Know

- Active fathering helps baby, dad, mom, and family.
- New father panic is completely normal—and survivable.
- Stay deeply involved in your child's life.
- Use the experience and wisdom of your family, heritage, and veteran fathers.

Preparing the Field

In This Chapter

- Building baby's nest
- Choosing a crib
- Gathering the essential gear and equipment
- Childproofing your life

In the weeks and months before the baby arrives, tons of people give you advice (often unsolicited) about what you need to do and what you need to buy. You see magazines in the doctor's office stuffed full of "essential" products every new baby has to have.

The hospital gives you a goody-bag full of freebies, ads, and coupons when you leave. You suddenly start noticing books, websites, news shows, and cable TV programs filled with advice about raising newborns and commercials for baby-related devices and gadgets you never imagined existed.

You have a lot of things to hunt for, gather, and put together. But it doesn't have to be an overwhelming minefield—as long as you avoid some of the hype.

Making a Nursery

In case you hadn't noticed, having a baby brings all kinds of changes to your life, including changes to your home and what you have inside it. You and your partner have some decisions to make.

The first one is where to put the baby.

> **HEADS UP**
>
> If you're not part of mom's life anymore, you still have practical contributions to make. Put aside conflicts to discuss with her how you can help provide the things your baby needs. Hint: a package of disposable diapers every month doesn't cut it. Helping to prepare the baby's room and equipment can set a pattern that helps you be part of your child's life for years to come.

Did it take a while for you and your partner to get used to each other once you started living together? That's normal; there's always a period of adjustment with a new roommate, whether in a dorm, apartment, or summer camp.

Well, your baby is unlike any roommate you've ever met. You can't negotiate or hold a mediation session with the baby. You sure can't take him to small claims court (at least not yet).

Thinking It Through

Your baby is pretty much dependent on you to meet his needs. You need to arrange and equip your home so you (and your partner) can do the job of taking care of him with as little distraction as possible; your child will provide infinite distractions on his own!

Let's start with four big picture rules for getting your home(s) ready for your baby:

- **Safety first.** And second, and third, and ... more on this later.
- **Don't bite off more than you can chew.** Time caring for and being with baby trumps polishing off a half-finished remodeling job.
- **Do it together.** Working with your partner on home prep can be fun, efficient, and creative. Honest!
- **Don't take yourself too damn seriously.** Pink vs. paisley on the nursery wallpaper trim isn't worth a skirmish with your partner or anyone else. By the time your child notices

the decorating choices, he'll be covering up the wallpaper with rock band posters, sports heroes, and whatever his generation's Harry Potter is.

We hear a lot about a mother's nesting instincts. Well, fathers have nesting instincts, too—just as we often have "sympathy" pains (called Couvade syndrome) during pregnancy. This makes sense when you remember that nature has known for eons that pregnancy and childbirth happen to two people, not just mom.

That's why many of us are drawn to remodeling a room into a nursery. Readying the baby's room is a concrete, fun, and manly way to express our nesting impulse.

Fortunately, preparing your home for the baby is an area where you can shine. If you have an ounce of organizational, painting, or other handyman skills, you can have a lot of fun and be very useful.

Choosing the Spot

The size and shape of your nursery (or the baby's room) depends a lot on the size and shape of where you live. Your baby won't care if the nursery is a multi-room suite or a tidy corner of the living room, as long as it is safe—and quiet, so he can sleep.

EXTRA POINT

Live-away dad? Make sure you have room in your living space to care for the baby when he is with you. It can be permanent or temporary; if temporary, just make sure you can set it up quickly and easily, and store it away neatly when you're done. Follow the "keep it simple; don't trip" principles that follow.

After you settle on the nursery's location, you can create a full-blown French provincial environment, with chandelier, life-sized stuffed poodle, framed baby dresses on the walls, wainscoting (Google it; I didn't know what it was, either), matching curtains, cross-stitched rocking chair upholstery, and hand-wrought crib curlicues. That's assuming you have tons of time and money.

If you're a schlub with a job and budget like the rest of us, then you'll do first things first: give the room a good scrubbing and assemble the furniture. If there's time left over, you might touch up the paint and fix the sticky window jamb.

However, your partner's preference may fall somewhere in between *House Beautiful* and *Handyman's Hovel*. Why? Because, unlike you and me, she has spent many hours (or years) dreaming about her baby's nursery.

It's another one of those boy-girl things. For example: How many childhood hours did you spend planning your wedding? That's what I thought.

It is always a bad idea to diss a woman's wedding plans, and you're asking for trouble if you ignore her nursery desires. Prepare to (a) compromise, and (b) completely agree on keeping the nursery (or nursery corner) safe and quiet. Quiet equals more baby sleep; and baby sleep is daddy and mommy's best friend.

Design and Layout

Lay out the room in a way that makes it completely safe for the baby and convenient for you. You'll do and juggle a lot in this space. So get some advice from other parents about what did and didn't work in their nursery or baby space. Brainstorm the setup with your partner to come up with ideas that will work for both of you.

When laying out the nursery, be sure to consider these factors:

- You and your partner's height
- Whether you and your partner are left- or right-handed
- The amount of light available over the diaper-changing surface
- The amount of light falling on the crib (less is better for sleeping)
- A floor surface that minimizes tripping and slipping
- Surfaces (from floor to ceiling) that you can clean easily

Keep the most-used things (crib and changing table, for example) within a short distance of each other. Before long, you'll be carrying your infant, diapers, lotion, bottles, pacifiers, stuffed animals, books, and who knows what else—all at once. The more steps you have to take, the more complicated and precarious things get.

So, keep it simple!

Check the Clock

Simple also means being reasonable about what you can and can't do before the baby arrives. For example, if you paint or lay new carpet, do it months before the baby is born (and keep your pregnant partner out of the room). New paint and wall-to-wall carpet can give off fumes that are unhealthy to pregnant women and infants. So, allow enough time (in the case of carpet, many weeks) for the fumes to leave the building. Blow a fan out the window to help things along. If it's winter, don't install new carpet if you can avoid it.

DAD WORDS

I would say my greatest achievement in life—and I'm still trying to achieve it—is to be a wonderful father to my kids.

—Bo Jackson

Notice the existing setup of the baby's space, and adapt to it. Don't put the crib near radiators or curtain cords, since they can pose a danger of burning or tangling up the baby. Don't put the changing table there, either. In fact, it might be best to avoid putting furniture on the same wall as the radiator and to eliminate window coverings that require cords. Bottom line; arrange everything with safety as a top priority.

Finally, have fun getting the room ready for your new little roommate (even if you have to work hard at it). Welcome your partner's involvement in the process, but don't be miffed if she suddenly doesn't have the interest or energy on a given day—remember, she's still pregnant.

Everything you do to prepare your child's new home is a contribution to your baby's happiness and good practice for a lifetime of supporting your child.

Sleeping Beauty

With any luck, your baby will spend more time in the nursery than you do—because she'll be asleep in there. Therefore, you have to make sure she's got something to sleep in. Simple, right? That's what you think.

Most friends and family mean well when they give you advice. A loved one is likely to speak with complete certainty about the superiority of crib A and urge you to avoid crib B at all costs.

And a week later, another relative or friend will tell you that crib B is the best, and crib A stinks.

Meanwhile, dozens of magazines, websites, and TV shows are out to make a few bucks by encouraging you (or scaring you) into buying their products and services.

Some of those items may be absolutely essential, and some may only seem that way.

Feel confused yet? Welcome to Buying for Baby! Hang on, though, it's not as bad as it sounds.

Cradles

Your infant spends more time sleeping than doing anything else, so you need a crib for him to do it in. Some parents like having a cradle first, when the infant is very young.

Whatever you choose, it has to be safe (of course). It also has to be built and positioned in a way that won't disrupt the baby's sleep. Those quiet moments are golden for you and him both after another round of feeding, pooping, playing, and crying.

Some experts frown on cradles: the March of Dimes recommends that you use a full-size crib, since bassinets and cradles don't have mandatory federal safety standards. But many parents use cradles comfortably and safely.

Make sure the cradle has a wide, stable base and a sturdy bottom. You also want a cradle that barely rocks. If it rocks too much, it can press your baby against the sides of the cradle. A safety sticker from the Juvenile Products Manufacturers Association (JPMA) is essential.

So-called co-sleepers (an infant bed that attaches to an adult bed) are more controversial than cradles, in part because there are no safety standards for co-sleepers. There are also concerns about how a parent might endanger the infant by moving around in his or her sleep.

Cribs

However you start out, your baby will end up in a crib for more than a year. Whether cradle, crib, or anything else, the safety issues fall into three general areas:

- How the item is constructed.
- What and how you put things (and the baby) in it.
- Where it is located.

On the question of construction, you want to be sure that the crib won't fall apart and that there's nothing for the baby's head or limbs to get caught in or tangled on. Look closely for splinters, rough edges, and other hazards, and then eliminate them.

Whether the crib is new or used, the U.S. Consumer Products Safety Commission (CPSC) says to make sure that it has adequate strength and stability in the frame and headboard, a secure fitting mattress support structure, and a label certifying that the crib complies with CPSC's latest standards for cribs.

The crib slats shouldn't be more than $2\frac{3}{8}$ inches apart—about the diameter of a soda can. Anything wider risks trapping a limb or head. (Plus, that distance is required by U.S. and Canadian law for all new cribs.) Don't use a crib if any slats are broken or missing.

You and your partner will reach into your baby's crib thousands of times. Make sure the side rail slides easily, but locks solidly in place when it's up. Also, set the mattress at a height that won't strain your back when bending over the crib. This may take some compromise, if one of you is substantially shorter than the other. (Yoga, anyone?)

Crib Assembly

Before putting the crib together, check that the hardware is all there and in good condition. When you assemble the crib, make sure all the pieces attach securely and the mattress fits snugly. (If there are parts left over, bad sign.)

All screws and bolts should fit tightly and not turn freely in the wood. If a screw cannot be securely tightened, replace it with a larger one that can. Also, check the wood joints to be sure they aren't coming apart.

Triple check that the mattress support hangers secure firmly to the hooks on the posts.

A crib headboard or footboard with cutout areas or designs may be beautiful to look at, but the baby's head can get trapped in those openings. Always choose safety over beauty.

If you use a hand-me-down or borrowed crib, make sure the corner posts don't reach higher than the rail. Those posts can snag a baby's clothes and cause strangulation. One simple solution is to saw off the posts (and then sand the ends to avoid splinters). If you can't or don't want to do that, get another (probably newer) crib.

 DAD WORDS

I felt something impossible for me to explain in words. Then, when they took her away, it hit me. I got scared all over again and began to feel giddy. Then it came to me … I was a father.

—Nat King Cole (on his daughter's birth)

Some older cribs (and older homes) have lead paint, which causes serious health problems like brain damage in infants and children. If you suspect that a hand-me-down crib might have lead paint, toss it in the trash. It isn't safe for any baby to use and it isn't even safe for an older child to play with.

If you ever have doubts about the condition of your crib, have it repaired or throw it out!

Crib Bling

Now that you have the crib assembled ... well, you're not done yet. Consider this a metaphor for fathering!

Use a teething cap on the side rail. This piece of plastic protects the top of the side rail from the baby's teeth—and protects him from splinters. Make sure that the cap fits snugly and doesn't have any cracks. He'll start chewing on it as soon as he can pull himself up, and his teeth are very strong (as your fingers will soon learn).

The most important thing you put in the crib is your child. The second most important thing is a firm mattress that fits snugly in the crib with no more than two fingers width (about an inch) between the edge of the mattress and the crib side. Also, some research indicates that a firm mattress reduces the incidence of Sudden Infant Death Syndrome (SIDS).

Use a fitted (not flat) sheet that is the right size to fit snugly over the mattress. You don't want any part of the baby tangled up in loose sheets or caught between the mattress and the sides of the crib (snug = safe). And in keeping with the snug theme: Be sure to have a snugly fitting waterproof pad underneath the sheet to protect the mattress.

 HEADS UP

Diapers leak and babies drool. Infancy is soggy. Deal with it.

Infants don't need pillows, quilts, or heavy blankets. Bedclothes increase the risk of tangling up the baby; pillows are a particular suffocation hazard. If a relative makes a beautiful comforter or quilt for the child, hang it on the wall or fold it safely away until your child is older and sleeping in her own bed.

Consider getting a bumper—padding around the ends and side rails of the crib—that keeps Little Ms. Squirm from bumping her head. Again, make sure the bumper is in good shape, fits snugly, and has nothing loose that she can catch herself on. Only use bumper pads until the child can pull herself up to a standing position. After she can stand, remove them so she can't use the pads to climb out of the crib. (Also ditch any mobiles once the baby can get herself into a standing position.)

Don't ignore what's outside the crib. Make sure there's nothing on the floor nearby (or anywhere in the room) that you'll trip over or slip on. That's a bad thing to do when carrying a baby when you're groggy in the middle of the night (or middle of the day!). Even if your hands are free, falling and breaking an arm will severely cramp your fathering style.

Don't put the crib near cords (electric, curtain, window shade, phone, and so on), window treatments (curtains, shades, and so on) or anything hanging down that the baby could get caught in. Don't put it right next to a radiator or fireplace—you don't want to burn the baby or yourself. (Believe me, you often lose track of your surroundings when you are tired and have an armful of baby.)

Unless your pediatrician tells you otherwise, a normal, healthy infant should always sleep on her back to reduce the risk of SIDS. Cover the baby with a thin covering, such as a crib blanket, receiving blanket, or other blankets specifically designed for infants. Don't pull a blanket up any farther than the baby's chest, and tuck the covering around the crib mattress. Swaddling can be good for newborns, but don't overdress your baby. Consider using a sleeper, wearable blanket, or other sleep clothing as an alternative to a covering.

Yes, there are a lot of warnings in crib land, but getting it right is important—and easier than it sounds.

The Rest of the Gear

In addition to sleeping, an infant spends a lot of time eating and drinking. Biological necessity means this will lead to a noticeable amount of peeing and pooping. (The censors won't let me be more graphic.)

Before these activities, the baby will often cry. You'll also notice crying during and after. If you have a baby that never cries, syndicate multiple media platforms so you can make millions telling other parents how to raise the perfect child.

Here are essentials you'll need in the nursery to facilitate feeding, sleeping, changing, and comforting your little one.

Changing Table

When you're at home, it's best to have a central location where you change the baby, dump her dumps, and keep all the necessary supplies. Most folks use a changing table for this and keep it in the nursery.

A store-bought changing table is nice, but not a necessity. You can adapt other solid furniture like tables, dressers, or chests into your baby-changing headquarters. No matter what you use, make safety come first.

A close second is adult convenience, which contributes to safety. If possible, choose a table whose "working surface" (the top, where you lay the baby down) is a good height for you and your partner.

EXTRA POINT

If you have more than one baby, you'll need more than one crib, car seat, infant seat, and so on. (You can get by with one changing table.) Don't be timid about borrowing and asking for help and/or gifts from relatives and friends. You may be surprised by how willing most people are to help—folks seem just captivated by twins and other multiples.

Make sure that there is *no* way that the baby can roll off while you're changing her. The working surface should have low sides and pad covering the area the baby lies in. Many changing tables come with a strap to help hold the baby in place—but you should always keep a hand on her no matter what.

Because we're dealing with diapers, the pad and/or its cover must be waterproof (duh).

The changing table should also have all of your supplies within very easy reach of one adult hand—because you always keep your other hand on the baby! You should be able to easily reach fresh diapers, wash cloths, baby wipes, skin ointment, and other materials. Yes, it's a lot to juggle—just think of diapering as preparation for all the other juggling you'll do as this kid grows up!

Oh, by the way, don't forget to buy diapers. Get a healthy supply of the right size before the baby comes home.

Diapering Decisions

That last instruction is more complicated than it sounds. Poop and pee are organic and biodegradable, but many diapers are not. This makes diapers a very hot topic. The three primary options each have their pros and cons:

Fully disposable. These have the most "in-the-moment" convenience. You take off the dirty one, slap on a new one, and throw the old one in the trash. If you care about the neighbors, you'll wrap it in a plastic bag on the way to the garbage can.

But fully disposables are less convenient for the planet. They count for as much as 2 percent of U.S. solid waste. Some manufacturers claim that their disposables are biodegradable, but it's hard to judge. Most disposables are about 30 percent plastic, which doesn't biodegrade.

In addition, the plastic parts of a disposable can irritate baby's skin, especially when it's hot and she's sweaty.

New reusables. These use a cloth cover (which functions like short shorts) with a liner made of paper or other mostly biodegradable fibers. You open up the cover, peel out (and toss) the liner, then insert a clean liner. Then, you wrap up the baby again: the cover usually has Velcro or other easy-to-use fasteners. Compared to standard disposables, they are slightly less convenient, but generate much less solid waste. They are also more expensive, although, you use the covers over and over (washing them occasionally!).

Old-fashioned reusable (a.k.a. cloth diapers). Cloth diapers work in most modern reusable diaper systems, fitting into the covers. Another (old school) option is using plastic pants to hold the diapers in place. On the plus side, you generate virtually no solid waste, the diapers last a very long time, and they are handy for many other purposes. A diaper service can also come every week and whisk away the dirty ones, if you can afford it—or receive diaper service as one of those ideal baby gifts.

On the down side, cloth diapers are messier to deal with and add a lot of water and detergent to the weekly laundry (either yours or the diaper service's). There are also environmental costs to manufacturing, distributing, and washing cloth diapers.

According to the University of Minnesota: "There is no clear answer as to which type of diaper is best for the environment over the total life cycle of the product." Different studies on diaper impact (paid for by different interests) produce different results. You'll have to make the call.

Rocking Chair

Infants and babies get great comfort from gentle movement. That's probably because they get used to nine months of gently floating around in momma's warm amniotic fluid.

A rocking chair or glider can help you provide relaxing movement for baby and for you—since babies are very quick to pick up on parental discomfort. Plus, why stand to rock the baby if there's a sitting option?

Some infants like movement while they eat, and others like to be still. Most babies go through phases where they like one way for a while, and then the other. A rocker gives you both options, whether it's mom breastfeeding or you bottle feeding. A little rocking usually helps the burping, too.

Most parents relax their infants for sleep by rocking (whether in a chair or carrying the baby around). Rockers are handy tools for many things baby—except for changing diapers!

Just like with cradles, avoid rocking chairs that go too far backward or forward; you don't want to tip over with the baby. Also, worrying about tipping over creates tension, which defeats the purpose of relaxing the baby.

Another option is a glider, which has a wood frame with cushions, and a series of hinges underneath that produce the smooth glide action. They often come with a gliding ottoman for your feet. Make sure the gliding mechanism doesn't squeak—the noise may not bother baby, but it may drive you crazy.

Finally, there's the wooden frame chair on traditional rockers. These often have a longer rocking angle, so test for your comfort and safety level. You'll also probably want cushions or some other padding for the baby's head—and your butt.

Infant Seat and High Chair

Infant seats and high chairs are essential once your baby starts eating solid food (solid is a relative term, as you soon learn), but they are handy to have from the beginning.

An infant seat has sides and holds the baby halfway between upright and totally reclined, so she can see things from a different perspective than when she's laying down or being held. This is a position many babies enjoy even before they can hold their heads up independently.

 DAD WORDS

I take my children everywhere, but they always find their way back home.

—Robert Orben

The best place to set an infant seat is on the floor, since there isn't far to fall over. You can also put one on a chair or couch, but the surface must always be a safe, stable location where you can keep a constant eye on her. Never put the baby in the seat without fastening the seat belt.

Don't use a high chair until the baby can sit up by herself, usually at six months or older. A high chair lets the baby sit near or at the kitchen or dining room table. It comes with a removable tray and a seat belt. Don't put the baby in the high chair without immediately fastening the seat belt (sound familiar?).

As with everything else, make absolutely sure that your infant seat and high chair are safe, meet current CPSC standards, and that you know how to operate them properly. Don't ever put a high chair on an unstable or uneven surface, let its screws or structure loosen, or use it as a stepladder.

The high chair tray and any areas where you feed your child will (100 percent guaranteed) get messy. Really messy. Hysterically messy. Food-fight messy. And that is entirely okay.

Messy is also developmentally necessary for your child. During her first 12 months (and well beyond), she learns by feeling, throwing, and otherwise playing with the things in front of her—including food. When she makes a mess with her food, she is not disrespecting you, doing performance art restaurant reviews, or showing bad manners—she is learning!

So go with the flow and don't stress about the mess. Instead, look at her behavior though the lens of learning. Think and talk about what she seems to be understanding about herself and her surroundings. Then clean up the mess and move on … with full knowledge that she's going to bring the mess again tomorrow!

Nursery Supplies

You need more than furniture to handle your baby. You also need some basic supplies:

Cloth diapers. Even if you only use disposable diapers on the baby's bottom, you'll need cloth ones (a lot of them) to wipe up things, put over your shoulder when burping, and do all sorts of other baby chores. They're soft, absorbent ways to gather the baby's bodily fluids (if you go for discreet terminology).

Changing paraphernalia. You'll need wipes, a washcloth, diaper rash ointment, baby powder, and toys (like a rattle or teething ring) to keep the baby distracted while you deal with poop, pee, and sore bottoms.

Feeding gear. Even if your partner is breastfeeding, you'll still need some bottles, nipples, and related paraphernalia. You may want a breast pump that gets mother's milk into a bottle, so you can feed and travel solo with the baby. Of course, if you use formula, you'll need a good supply of bottles and formula.

Diaper bag. It doesn't matter what brand or shape you use—or even if the bag was designed for diapers. It's the essential baby care toolbox. Just make sure you never leave home without a large, easy-to-carry bag. Most parents carry diapers (both disposable and cloth); a waterproof pad you can lay the baby on anywhere (park lawn, shag carpet, car hood, and so on); wipes, ointment, diaper covers, plastic pants, and any other regular items you use at home to change a diaper; pacifiers; bottles; and small toys.

Bath Gear

Did I mention that babies make messes while eating? And while burping, peeing, pooping? Good—you got that.

As a result, babies also need baths fairly often—in a place that won't endanger him or you.

If you have a bathtub, great. If not, you can rig up an arrangement in or near the kitchen sink. Either way, it helps to have a bath seat, bath sling, or baby tub. Most options are inexpensive inflatable or plastic mini-tubs or recliners that you can set inside a bathtub or large sink or else set up on a counter or other stable, flat surface next to a sink.

Just be sure to put the bath seat where the baby can't reach the faucet or spout. If the bath seat moves or tips while your child is in it, stop using it. Unplug any nearby small appliances (blow dryers, razors, and irons) and keep them out of the baby's reach.

Never leave the baby unattended in or near the water. If you need to leave the bath area, take the baby with you. Don't rely on older children to watch him for you.

DAD WORDS

I knew I was an unwanted baby when I saw that my bath toys were a toaster and a radio.

—Joan Rivers

Baby soap, baby shampoo, and super-soft towels and washcloths make bathing your baby safe and even fun. Be sure to collect all of your bathing gear before bringing baby into the bathroom (so you don't have to leave him unattended to retrieve a missing item).

After running a minimum amount of warm water in the tub, carefully place baby into the bath seat and go to work. The water temperature shouldn't be too hot or too cold (is Goldilocks in the house?), but if you're not sure, go for cooler over hotter. You can buy a baby bathwater thermometer, but you can easily, quickly, and more cheaply learn how to use your hand (and common sense) to gauge the heat—especially with a minute of coaching from one of your parents or another veteran parent.

Finally, when your child can pull himself to a standing position, it's time to put away the bath seat or baby tub. From then on, wash him in a regular tub—and work on your bag of tricks to keep him amused and distracted while you get the job done.

Childproofing the House

Childproof your entire home as soon as possible. Before you know it, he'll be a toddler exploring electric outlets with his fingers and crawling into the cupboard where you store the drain cleaner.

Like many other preparations for baby, you need to examine the big picture, and get down (literally) into the little-bitty details.

Take a look at your entire living situation. Are the major appliances functioning properly and safely? Are there problems (like a loose board on the front porch) that you work around without even noticing anymore?

Next, you need to get down on the floor and pretend you are a crawling baby or running toddler. What actual or potential safety hazards do you see from the low-down perspective?

Take dangerous things that are reachable (chemicals, household cleaners, medications, tools, tacks, nails, and so on) and make them unreachable. And do it before the baby is born.

Most hardware, department, and toy stores have the childproofing materials you'll need. Keep in mind that many of these child-proofing tools will be in place for five years or more, so get ones that will last.

Smoke Alarm

Make sure you have a fully functioning smoke alarm on each floor of your home, or near key areas of your apartment. Follow the smoke alarm's instructions to find the best locations.

Need a simple way to keep the batteries fresh? Change them on the two weekends when we start and stop daylight savings time. Arizona, Hawaii, or Saskatchewan don't observe DST, so if you live there, come up with another method—and let us know when we can come visit!

It is also an excellent idea to have a functioning home fire extinguisher on each floor. Put it somewhere easy for you (but not baby) to reach and where you will remember to find it in an emergency.

Your local fire department has information about smoke alarms and fire extinguishers, and may even have a program to help you purchase them. Even if you live in a small apartment, don't live without a smoke alarm.

DAD WORDS

What a dreadful thing it must be to have a dull father.

—Mary Mapes Dodge

The Kitchen

Start by putting childproof outlet covers on every electrical outlet in the kitchen—and the rest of your home. Kids of all ages (including crawling babies) like picking one thing up and sticking it into something else. If he puts a nail in a socket, you've got trouble.

Install locks on your cupboard and cabinets. These small, flexible plastic devices go inside a cabinet door, and keep kids from opening it more than an inch or two.

Until you and mom master their use, child safety devices may keep you from opening the door, too, but be patient and you'll get the hang of it. ("Be patient and you'll get the hang of it" sounds like a pretty good motto for everything about being a parent.) The locks are made for both sliding and hinged doors. You can also get childproof latches for appliances like the dishwasher and fridge.

Don't forget drawer latches. They function like cabinet locks.

Use sponge tape or other secure padding to cover sharp edges that an infant or crawling baby can bang into, whether in the kitchen or anywhere else. Make sure there are no loose ends or other spots that he can start eating.

Keep the baby away from the open doors of a refrigerator or dishwasher; you don't want things falling on him or little fingers pinched in the hinges.

Always monitor the stove and oven, keeping baby at a distance when those (or any other appliances) are turned on. Make sure the handles of all pots and pans—whether on the stove or any other surface—are turned inward. You don't want the child (or your clothing) to grab the handle and spill hot things on the kid. For extra precaution, consider lock covers for the knobs on your stove and range.

Just like you did in the nursery, get all cords and cord-like things (like aprons) out of baby's reach. Roll-up devices for window cords are handy.

Put bright stickers on glass doors, so neither the baby nor you (when you're distracted) run into them.

Put up a refrigerator magnet or other easily visible sign with emergency phone numbers and instructions for baby first aid, CPR, and choking.

Living Areas

Yes, the baby will spend most of her time eating and sleeping. But you will want to show her off—and eventually, she'll be scooting around on her own. So, you have to get the rest of the house ready, too.

If your home has any stairs, one or more safety gates will make life much easier. These portable gates keep a baby from crawling, rolling, or falling through a doorway or down to the next floor. You can move them around the house, and they bring great peace of mind.

It may seem like your child continuously outwits you with all the things she gets into. But she's not trying to show you up; she's just exploring. If there's some possession you really value—say, your TV and audio equipment—childproof it. A few years back, my friend's toddler put a remote control into the VCR player's tape slot. Seemed logical to the kid, but dad and mom never could fish it back out. One more reason to cheer the demise of VCRs.

In the bathroom, think about grip tape or gripping stickers for the floor of the bathtub (or sink, if you use it for bathing) to help prevent the baby from sliding around while soaped up. They help you stay on your feet, too.

Make sure the bathroom also has a functioning baby thermometer to take his temperature. If you're a middle-aged new dad, don't freak out; anal thermometers are rare now. The new models (like the pacifier that doubles as a thermometer!) are high-tech and easier to use than when we were kids.

The baby will spend time in your bedroom (ideally, when you're not having sex), so make sure it's well childproofed, too. Secure the outlets, closets, drawers, and doors. You can also get grips to put over doorknobs, making them easier for you to turn while carrying an infant.

The Least You Need to Know

- You need to prep for baby before she comes.
- Your baby's space must (and can) be safe.
- When it comes to planning the baby's nursery, be willing to compromise with mom; she's probably been thinking about this for a lot longer than you have.
- Getting the house ready for baby can be fun.

Away Games

In This Chapter

- Taking baby on the road
- Making trips safe
- Budgeting for baby
- Parenting together and apart

Even if you never plan to visit friends or relatives (bad idea, should you value your sanity), you will have to take baby to the doctor and on errands.

Now that you have your home field ready for the baby, it's time to prepare yourself and your partner for taking the baby out of the house. You want to make those trips safely and smoothly—understanding that smooth trips are a highly relative concept in baby land. That means getting essential gear and sorting through a lot of advice and hype.

Buyer Beware

Right now, you might feel overwhelmed by all the stuff you're supposed to have, the advice you get, and the marketing pitches you see. And that's on top of the sensations you may be having just because you are—or are about to be—a new father!

In this chapter, I help you sort out what's absolutely essential and what only seems that way—always keeping in mind that your new child's most vital need is you!

You probably don't fall for everyday marketing hype, but you may feel differently when it comes to protecting your new child and making sure he gets every opportunity possible. Your fears and concerns are natural—and great opportunities for outfits selling baby gear.

Times like this call for an age-old cliché: if it sounds too good to be true, it probably is.

No baby toy or tool will get your child a) potty trained at 3 months, b) the starting point guard slot in high school, and c) early admission into M.I.T. (or your money back!). As with most things in life (and in fathering), a healthy supply of common sense is the best defense.

EXTRA POINT

An excellent resource for parents is the nonprofit Campaign for a Commercial-Free Childhood (commercialfreechildhood.org). They have tips and information to help you sniff out the B.S. in marketing pitches and great ideas on stimulating your child's development with simple, inexpensive toys, tools, and strategies.

Parenting author Pamela Paul says any baby product can seem logical or necessary at some moment of parental distress and concern. But we have to know when someone is pushing our buttons and trying to take advantage of our new parent insecurity.

Fatherly caution is useful, but parenting from fear is a mistake. So don't buy into the idea that "If I don't buy baby gear X, something terrible will happen to my baby." Just remember all of the geniuses of the past and present who succeeded before the days of retail baby registries! I've said it before, and I'll say it again: your baby needs you far more than he needs any stuff you can buy.

Car Seat

Because your baby will spend time in a motor vehicle, a car safety seat is a must-have item.

A car seat forms a protective barrier that absorbs the force of a crash. Because the seat is strapped down, it also keeps your baby from flying around inside the car during a collision. Never put a child in any kind of vehicle without a functioning, correctly installed child safety seat.

When it's pouring rain and you're late for dinner at Grandpa's house, getting the baby settled in his car seat seems like a huge hassle. True, it is a hassle. But it's a far smaller hassle than years of grief and/or hospitalization if he's thrown around the vehicle in an accident.

Why Use One?

The biggest remaining factor in child death and injuries on the road? Adults who don't put their kids in car seats.

Child safety seats are fairly new on the scene. During my mid-1950s infancy, our Desoto didn't even have seatbelts, so I slept in an unsecured backseat bassinette (basically, a glorified basket). Yes, this dates me as an official old fart, but it wasn't long ago that a space capsule was the only vehicle with seatbelts.

Thanks to changes in government policy, the number of U.S. and Canadian children killed in car accidents has dropped dramatically in the last 40 to 50 years, as seatbelts and child safety seats became mandatory.

HEADS UP

Aside from your child's safety, it is against the law in every U.S. state and Canadian province to drive an infant in a vehicle without securing him in a car seat. Plus, a hospital won't let you take the baby home unless your car has a properly installed, fully functioning car seat—and the baby is in it!

No matter how strong you are, your strength alone can't protect your child during an accident. It is simply not safe to hold your child in your arms in a car. At speeds as low as 30 MPH your child can be ripped from your arms in a crash and crushed between your body and the windshield or dashboard.

How to Use One

From birth through 12 months, your child should always ride in a rear-facing car seat. "Infant-only" seats only face the rear, and don't convert for use when the baby is older.

So-called "convertible" and "combo" car seats have additional settings that adjust when your child is large enough to move to a front-facing position. In addition, they typically have higher height and weight limits for the rear-facing position, allowing you to keep your child rear-facing for a longer period of time.

Never put a child safety seat in the front seat of a vehicle. Air bags (required in cars, SUVs, and vans since 1998) are dangerous for babies and younger children. Air bags inflate almost instantly after a crash (even just a fender bender) and can explode out of the dashboard at 200 miles per hour. That can save an adult's life, but kill a baby.

A rear facing car seat puts the infant's head toward the front of the vehicle. If the car seat is in the car's front seat, the baby's head is directly in the air bag's line of fire.

The ideal location for any car seat is in the center of the vehicle's backseat. Avoid driving your baby in pickup trucks or sports cars that don't have a backseat.

After his first birthday, keep your child rear-facing as long as possible. Your child shouldn't move up to a new position until he reaches the top height or weight limit allowed by your car seat's manufacturer. Once your child outgrows the rear-facing car seat, he's ready to travel in a forward-facing car seat with a harness.

Most kids stay in a car seat until about age four; the determining factor in "moving up" is weight.

You can get an infant-only car seat for about $80 and can spend hundreds on a high-end combination model (more on these in the next section). Fortunately, many hospitals offer programs where you can rent a child safety seat for the first few years of your child's life. Some car and health insurance companies have occasional free or discounted car seat offers, too. Call yours and ask.

If you try to save money by borrowing a car seat from a friend or family member (or buying one on Craigslist), make absolutely sure that ...

- It hasn't passed its expiration date. That is usually 5 or 6 years from the date the seat was manufactured (not the day it was first purchased).
- It isn't broken or damaged, even a little bit.
- You know the proper way to install the seat in the car.
- You know the proper way to strap your baby in the car seat.

DAD WORDS

If the new American father feels bewildered and even defeated, let him take comfort from the fact that whatever he does in any fathering situation he has a 50 percent chance of being right.

—Bill Cosby

The National Highway Traffic Safety Administration (NHTSA) regulates car seats and has excellent, easy-to-use information about them. Check nhtsa.gov/Safety/CPS if you have any questions about whether the seat you have will work. Or call the NHTSA Auto Safety Hotline at 800-424-9393 (800-424-9153 for people with hearing impairments).

New child safety seats include a manufacturer's registration form; fill it out and send it in so that the manufacturer can reach you if they ever issue a safety recall on your model.

If you have any doubts about a used car seat, invest in a new one; your child's life is worth it.

Combo, Cash, and Convenience

Combo seats allow you to pull the seat out of the car without having to unstrap the baby from the seat. (In other words, you move the seat, not the baby.) You can then use the combo as an infant seat in the house, or snap it into a stroller and wheel away. Of course, the more components you have, the more expensive your combo is.

The combo sets do have advantages. Some parents prefer their bulk to repeatedly buckling and unbuckling the baby. Just be aware that each option you choose also tends to make the thing larger and heavier. When the stroller starts looking like a Humvee, it is hard to get through narrow doorways and into tight spaces.

HEADS UP

Never put a child in any kind of vehicle if he isn't properly strapped into a functioning, correctly installed child safety seat. Period. It isn't worth the risk. Not even once.

You can spend less than $100 by getting a convertible model that isn't a combo. You can use one of these as a rear-facing seat until your child is about 20 pounds. Then you can convert it to a front-facing seat that keeps him safe until he is 40 pounds.

Strollers

Strollers are vital for getting the baby around any public place, the street, and even your own home (unless you have extraordinary upper body strength, stamina, and will always be on call to carry the baby). In addition, the movement of a stroller is both stimulating and soothing to him.

The simplest, fold-up umbrella stroller costs less than $40, and you can spend $700 on the highest-end jogging strollers. Don't make an impulse purchase or get caught in a seductive sales pitch and buy more than you need; think through your situation and purchase accordingly.

Balance price, maneuverability, weight, and repetition of your daily car seat- and stroller-related tasks. There are simple steps to factor in the basics.

Test drive different models (especially car seat-stroller combos) in the store and, if possible, around the shopping mall. For example, wheel the stroller into an often-crowded space (like a Starbucks or supermarket). How easy is it to get around? (My daughter—a new mom and veteran barista—wishes coffee-drinking parents would leave their strollers outside!)

Examine how many components are adjustable. Does everything snap into positions that accommodate the height and reach of 1) momma, 2) you, 3) other adults wheeling baby around frequently?

Is the frame easy for you, your partner, or other adults to lift and maneuver? Measure the stroller's dimensions (open and collapsed) to make sure it easily fits into, and moves smoothly around, your house. Then, check to see if it fits the vehicle(s) you use to transport the baby. How easily does the stroller fold up to fit on public transportation?

Discuss with your partner how much storage space (pouches, pockets, and cup holders) you'll need on a stroller. Be sure to evaluate how filling up the storage space affects the stroller's balance and maneuverability.

If the sidewalks in your neighborhood are rough, or you'll be traveling a lot with the baby, make sure the stroller is sturdy enough to take the punishment. If you're a marathoner (what are you thinking? You have a new baby!!!), you'll need a heavier-duty jogging stroller for your runs, and a smaller one for getting around the house and the grocery store.

Whether you're buying or borrowing, safety is a top priority. The Juvenile Products Manufacturers Association (JPMA) says that the stroller must have a base wide enough to prevent tipping, even when your baby leans over the side. If the seat reclines, the stroller must not tip backward when she lies down.

EXTRA POINT

Many new parents rely on jogging strollers to help them stay in physical shape. These heavy-duty three-wheeled jobs can handle rougher surfaces and keep the baby safe at slightly higher speeds than a lighter stroller. When with the baby, stay on low-traffic, residential streets.

Be sure you know how to operate your stroller correctly. Always secure the baby by using the stroller harness. Never hang pocket-books, knapsacks, or shopping bags over the handles—the stroller could tip backward. Always use the locking device to prevent accidental folding and apply the brakes to keep the stroller from rolling away. (Did I mention the importance of common sense?) When you (or any other adult) fold or unfold the stroller, watch for pinched fingers—yours and baby's.

Never let a young child push your infant in the stroller without close and constant supervision. Be aware of your surroundings and use your head; keep the stroller close when in a parking lot or crossing a street, and don't let go of it on a hill.

The JPMA has a comprehensive list of safety steps and considerations on its Safety House website: www.jpma.org/content/parents/safety-house.

Play Pens, a.k.a. Play Yards

Are play pens called *play yards* now because it sounds classier somehow? Who knows, but I'm quite sure that your baby will have no concept of classy when he's inside that thing-a-ma-jig.

The play yard is a contained area that the baby can play or nap in. When he's ready, he will pull himself up to a standing position in there to see what's going on and to interact with you.

As with car seats and strollers, you can pay anywhere from $60 to $300 (and more) for play yards. And as with other baby equipment, always make safety and usability your top priorities. Is the play yard sturdy enough so that it doesn't wiggle or start to flip when the baby moves around (and especially stands up) in it? Is it simple to set up, fold up, and transport from place to place?

Today's play yards have mesh siding to prevent fingers, limbs, and heads from getting caught anywhere. Make sure the mesh holes are no larger than $\frac{1}{4}$ inch. (If you use a hand-me-down wooden play pen, be sure the slats are no more than $2\frac{3}{8}$" apart.) Play yards also have snug fitting, waterproof mats on the bottom, which come in handy if you're away from home and put the baby down for a nap in there.

A few other common sense basics, courtesy of JPMA:

- Erect the play yard, including side rails, securely and fully before use.
- Don't put extra padding or any other objects inside the play yard that might give your child the ability to climb out.
- When he's in there playing, don't leave him unattended.
- Don't suspend strings or ropes over the play yard or attach strings to toys inside it.

Carrying Contraptions

Never doubt parental creativity. Our inventive spirit created the hundreds of ways to carry babies around. From the papoose to the Moby, mom and dad have always sought an easier, softer way to lug that kid.

One popular method is a long piece of fabric that parents must learn the mysteries of folding around themselves and the baby. For example, the Moby Wrap requires a 7-step procedure.

Other baby carriers use backpack-like straps with a pouch that has holes for the baby's feet. You wear some models on your front, with the baby facing inward toward you (ideal for snuggling) or outward toward the world (great for seeing baby's reactions and showing him off).

Other models have the pouch in the back, but wait to use one of those until the baby can hold his head up for a good amount of time. Finally, some car seats have a detachable assembly that lets you carry the baby like he's in a basket.

Climate Considerations

You have to dress for the weather, and so does your baby. How you dress can be a good guide for dressing your baby. But be sure to tune in to your baby's own rhythms (especially skin and body temperature) to make sure you're keeping him safe and comfortable.

Hot Times

In warm weather, use light and breathable clothing. Light colors help, since they help reflect the sun. Whenever possible, stick to cotton fabrics, since synthetics can irritate the baby's skin and contribute to overheating.

Babies are more susceptible to rapid changes in temperature, so protect against chills with a blanket or sweater when going from outdoor heat into air conditioning.

The sun's rays can damage the skin of babies and young children and increase the risk of skin cancer later in life. This is true regardless of the baby's skin color. Black babies get sunburn and black adults get skin cancer.

However, sunscreen isn't your best bet before six months. Using sunscreen too early can increase the chances of an allergic reaction, which limits your options when he's older. When he's that young, simply keep the baby out of direct sunlight as much as you can. Dress him with a brimmed hat, long sleeve top, and long cotton pants.

A stroller hood or umbrella can also protect the baby on sunny days. Bottom line: any part of your baby that is uncovered in the sun may get sunburned.

When baby is past six months, it's still wise to check with your pediatrician before using sunscreen. The American Academy of Dermatology recommends a broad-spectrum sunscreen of SPF 15 or higher for everyone, regardless of skin color. To reduce potential problems for the baby, use products that are hypoallergenic, fragrance free, and easy to apply.

The sun can also strain or damage baby's eyes. So use baby sunglasses on bright days. No need to spend a fortune; simple plastic ones will do. He'll pull them off and fuss about them at first, but most kids get used to them eventually.

If the baby is in a baby carrier, check regularly to see how hot he's getting. The heavier your baby carrier's fabric, the greater the chance he'll overheat (even when it's cold out).

READING THE SIGNS

Babies can't regulate their body temperature as well as older children, so pay attention!

When it's hot, both you and the baby should drink extra fluids—but don't give him sports drinks, soda, or other sugar- and salt-laden liquids. Stick to water, diluted juice, or breast milk.

Cold Calls

Your baby will get cold faster than you will, so approach cold weather accordingly. Those of us with long years in northern climes know the value of layers. Using just a single layer of clothing or covering (like a blanket) on the baby won't work for long. Any opening lets in the chill, and one heavy layer can quickly produce overheating—which later leads to chills.

The SIDS Center of the University of Minnesota (where they know winter) says, "Your baby is overheated if he is sweating, has damp hair, a heat rash, rapid breathing, or is restless."

Sweaters are effective and versatile layering tools. Make sure you have several, because baby will spit up on them; soggy clothing stinks at keeping him warm … and will sometimes just stink, period.

You can use a knit hat, mittens, and warm socks no matter where you live. For example, Arizona's evening air can give baby a chill just as easily as a Manitoba morning. If you live someplace (like Minnesota or Manitoba) where winter means winter, then you'll need a snow suit for going outside. Just remember that the snow suit covers other, layered clothing—don't put him in there naked!

When he's sleeping, use a sleep sack or footed sleeper to keep baby warm. This gives him a little room to move around, while capturing heat without multiple layers. You want as few layers as possible when changing a diaper in the middle of the night.

HEADS UP

Make absolutely sure that any loaners, hand-me-downs, and secondhand purchases meet current safety standards and haven't been recalled for defects by a manufacturer. The U.S. Consumer Products Safety Commission maintains a thorough list of Infant/Child Product Recalls at: cpsc.gov/cpscpub/prerel/category/child.HTML (or call 800-638-2772).

The Least You Need to Know

- Buying more stuff doesn't make you a better father.
- Common sense and online resources can help you shop smartly for the equipment you and baby need.
- Managing your baby and his gear is work, but well worth the effort.
- It's okay to buy used baby gear as long as it's safe and in good shape.

Drafting Personnel

In This Chapter

- Choosing doctors and other professionals
- Exploring your daycare options
- Keeping your parents helpful
- Sharing parenting duties

When was the last time you chose an obstetrician, watched a baby be born (live, not on YouTube), searched for child care providers, or defended your parenting style?

If you successfully did all four of these before your partner got pregnant, why do you need this book? But nearly every expectant and new dad has to face these questions for the first time.

In this chapter, I help you scout for and build a birth and infancy support team that will give you a winning record.

OBs, Midwives, and Other Aliens

Let's assume you've never been to a gynecologist. Well, you need to know how valuable your support and advocacy are for your partner now as you enter the world of OB/GYNs and the many strangers you need on this journey.

You and your partner need a doctor (usually an obstetrician/gynecologist, or OB/GYN) or a certified nurse-midwife with experience delivering babies. Many family practice doctors or general practitioners also oversee a woman's pregnancy and deliver babies. However, they always have an OB/GYN on call in case complications arise.

READING THE SIGNS

A *perinatologist* is an obstetrician who specializes in treating women with special medical problems during pregnancy, due to her heredity, chronic illnesses, or other factors.

This doc will be your primary resource on the health of your partner and your soon-to-be-baby. If the OB/GYN is the doctor your partner sees now for her "lady issues," then they may already have a good relationship.

If not, then it's important for you to participate in choosing your OB/GYN. Either way, you need to participate in your partner's health care up to and beyond the day of birth.

In addition to a doctor, some new parents also decide to use a certified nurse-midwife (CNM) or a doula.

A midwife is not the bride between marriage number 1 and marriage number 3. CNMs are masters-degree registered nurses with specialized training (and state licenses) in obstetrics. Most work with hospitals and have a network of anesthesiologists, neonatologists, and OB/GYNs to call on if complications arise.

Nurse-midwives tend to be less formal and more family centered than a traditional OB/GYN. For example, they will often support a home-based birth. If there aren't complications or high risks in the pregnancy, CNMs can be an excellent way to go. Learn more from The American College of Nurse-Midwives at acnm.org.

A doula is not an exotic bird or the title of a doo-wop song. Doulas (usually women) give emotional and physical support to a pregnant woman and her partner during labor, delivery, and afterward.

She is not a medical professional, but is trained to ease the discomfort of pregnancy and labor with massage, aromatherapy, comfort, and the wisdom and knowledge drawn from past experience. In other words, she fills the role played for centuries by older female relatives and neighbors.

University of Toronto nursing Professor Dr. Ellen D. Hodnett studied 13,000 pregnant women and found that those using the support of non-medical companions like doulas had fewer complications during labor and were less likely to need epidurals or C-sections (head over to Chapter 7 for details on these procedures).

Making Your Pick

Picking an OB/GYN (or CMM or doula) is kind of like drafting a pitching corps. You'll spend a fair amount of time together with these professional teammates, the most intense being at the very end. So you should get along.

Like a good teammate, your OB/GYN doesn't necessarily have to be the kind of person you'd marry. On the other hand, she shouldn't be the kind of person you despise, either.

Basically, you want to find someone who understands, respects (and, perhaps, shares) your values—someone you can communicate with. Don't let other people railroad you into what they think is the best draft pick—do what's best for you and your partner.

If you two like being in charge and think the doctor should be more of a colleague than anything else, fine. If, because the doctor went to med school, you think you should leave all the decisions in his hands, that's fine, too—as long as it suits what you need. The goal here is not to prove anything to anyone—it's to have a healthy baby.

The Cleveland Clinic suggests asking these practical questions when seeking a health care provider:

- How long have you been in practice?
- When and where did you receive training?
- Are you board-certified? Do you have references?
- Have you had any problems with your medical practice? (Your state medical licensing board may have this information.)

- What is your pregnancy, labor, and delivery philosophy? (Think about how that fits in with your own beliefs.)
- How many babies do you deliver per week?
- Do you have children?
- Are you in a group practice? If so, do we have a choice of who we see and who actually delivers our baby?
- Will you be in town around our due date? (No one doctor is awake and available 24/7, so be sure you know which colleague(s) might end up delivering your baby—and make sure those colleagues know what you want when the time comes.)
- If we have a question, who do we call? Who responds to the calls? Do you accept questions via email or text?
- Do you induce labor if we go beyond our due date?
- What criteria do you use when deciding to do a caesarian?
- Can and will you deliver the baby in the facility we want to use?
- How do you feel about working with a midwife and/or doula?

If a trained, professional doctor seems insulted by this kind of interrogation, that's a bad sign; move on to someone else.

Be aware of how the doctor answers your questions (body language, tone of voice, and so on) as well as the words she uses. If you trust the doctor's style, that's a real plus.

Med school professor Joy Dorscher, MD, has delivered hundreds of babies. She says, "When you get right down to it, parents don't really need me there most of the time; nature knows how to deliver a baby. But when they do need me (because baby or mother are in trouble), then they really need me."

Dorscher's philosophy for working with expectant parents is simple: "I'll do everything you want as long as I can, but then you need to let me do what I need to do when I have to do it. That's my job."

Some veteran parents (and even some doctors and nurses) suggest that you get recommendations from the nursing staff at the hospital you're using. Those nurses see the doctors at peak stress times and know which ones are best at listening to and respecting what parents-to-be want.

Enough Tests—This Is No Peepshow!

As a good partner and father, you should attend OB/GYN appointments with your partner; however, don't be surprised if you find the experience upsetting. Here's a perfect stranger (sometimes a man) peering and poking into her genitalia, ordering tests for her blood, urine, STD history—even mammograms! You may want to push the doc away, shouting "Hands off! That's my woman!"

I have news for you. Outside business hours, nearly every gynecologist (regardless of their sex) will tell you that any titillation there might have been in a pelvic or breast examination is long gone by the time a doctor leaves medical school. Looking into a stranger's vagina quickly loses its allure when you do it 120 times a week, every week.

Your doctor-visit presence has many practical benefits. It's hard to stay mentally sharp when someone is examining your cervix or hooking up medical equipment on your belly. Mom can easily forget questions she wanted to ask or important information she wanted to pass along. That's where you come in.

Make sure you write down questions and details before you leave home. Then make sure the doctor answers all of her questions—and yours.

Don't put up with doctors or others treating you like a fifth wheel or dissing your partner, but be polite. If you've been waiting in the examination room for a half hour, be the one who goes and finds out why.

As a new dad, develop your ability to speak up for what you think is best, and simultaneously be open to compromise—especially with your partner. You'll be doing this parenting thing together for a long time.

So whether you're dealing with your partner or her caregivers, communicate, communicate, and then communicate some more.

Your First Visit

Alert! Do *not* miss the first OB/GYN appointment, because it's the most important one. The first visit is usually longer than other visits because the doctor needs to get a medical history (if he doesn't already have one) and assess your partner's health and health risks.

At the first visit, you'll get asked (both of you) whether you've had any sexually transmitted diseases, been exposed recently to contagious diseases like measles, and whether you smoke. Your partner will need to tell about previous medical problems and what drugs she's taking (both prescription and over-the-counter).

The OB/GYN will want to know whether you or your partner have a family history of chronic illness or genetic abnormalities. You'll also be asked about diseases common to your ethnic background, such as sickle cell anemia in African Americans.

You can ask questions, too—about your due date, diet and nutrition, exercise, what symptoms are normal, whether your partner is at risk for any problems during pregnancy, and so on.

This is one doctor's visit when you want to be sure to write down your list of questions the night before. In the excitement of "our first appointment," it's easy to forget some of the things you were sure you were going to ask. This visit is also the time to ask "who do I call in your office when we have questions between appointments?"

Being part of the OB/GYN world makes things more real for you as a dad and helps you prepare psychologically for fatherhood. At the doctor's office, you'll have your first look at the baby as a grainy, swimming image on the sonogram machine. You'll hear the baby's heartbeat a lot sooner if you have the doctor's stethoscope.

But you can't experience any of that if you don't show up. And one of the first rules of fathering is "Show Up."

Pink, Blue, Up to You

Most expectant parents get several sonograms, or ultrasounds, during the pregnancy to identify problem conditions in the mother and the baby. Sonograms also help determine the date you got pregnant, whether you're having more than one child, fetal heartbeat, location of the placenta and fetus—and the sex of your baby.

Although the technician or doctor may sometimes miss the penis or no-penis call, the bigger question is: do you want to know the baby's sex before she or he is born?

Before my daughter and son-in-law had their ultrasound, they asked my advice on the "should we know?" question. I favored the old-fashioned way: find out when the baby is born. My wife's advice? "Find out and tell me right away; I want to know!" Figures.

Why find out before delivery? If you want to pick only one name, or you're determined to make the baby's nursery and wardrobe pink or blue now (FYI, 100 years ago, pink was the boy's color because it represented blood and virility).

Plus, if we have the technology, why not find out?

Why wait? Because that's how it's been done for millennia; you like surprises, you can still dream about either sex (which may help distract you during pregnancy's last weeks). You may enjoy torturing your relatives and friends.

You can also annoy relatives and friends by finding out yourselves, but not telling anyone else.

The most important factor is making your decision together. Talk openly about the pros and cons, make a decision, and then respect each other by sticking to it.

Do I Have to Watch the Bloody Birth?

If you don't want to be in the delivery room for the birth of your baby, make your feelings known well ahead of time. It's estimated that 10 to 20 percent of men choose not to participate in the delivery for reasons ranging from personal to religious.

You may be afraid that you'll panic, be sick at the sight of blood, or just feel too overwhelmed. You may think you won't be able to stand seeing your partner in great pain, or witness potential problems with the baby.

EXTRA POINT

Mayo Clinic researchers say that new dads worry about the health of their babies nearly as obsessively as new mothers do. According to the researchers, 58 percent of new fathers admitted having some form of irrational fear or thoughts about their new infants.

You may also think that your presence invades your partner's privacy, since childbirth is such a personal and intimate event. You might also feel like you don't belong because labor and delivery are jobs best left to women alone. Or she may tell you that she doesn't want you there.

You may also worry that your manhood will be challenged by reversing traditional gender roles; you'd give the encouragement and emotional support while your partner courageously toughs it out through the stress and pain.

Religious beliefs can also determine your decision. Some Hindu, Orthodox Jewish, and African religious sects disapprove of men witnessing childbirth. These traditions view childbirth as unclean, requiring purification of mother and child—tasks other women perform.

You and your partner need to discuss your feelings, fears, and beliefs openly before you get to labor and delivery day. Your child's birth is an emotional and unique event—there are no do-overs. So before making this decision, give it good, hard consideration.

You will find considerable wisdom if you talk it over with other fathers. Few men love the sight of blood, but few notice it—or stay squeamish for long—in the excitement of childbirth itself.

Most women want their partners in the room. You know her well, so you can respond quickly to her needs. Many couples feel an immense sense of intimacy, wonder, and spiritual connection during and immediately after childbirth. Plus, while witnessing your child's first moments of life, you'll start a lifelong bond.

If, in the end, you decide to patrol the waiting room instead of the delivery room, your partner may feel disappointed. Don't blame her or fight with her about those feelings. And don't blame yourself, either. You're not a failure if don't see your child born; you can still bond with him and be there every other step of the way with and for your partner and child.

Finding the Right Pediatrician

After she's born, your child needs a doctor who specializes in the prevention and treatment of childhood health problems. You and your child will probably visit her pediatrician for a lot longer than you and your partner saw the OB/GYN—many years vs. a few months. So, just like with choosing the OB/GYN, make sure to find a pediatrician you get along with.

Health care experts encourage parents to pick a pediatrician (or at least do the research) before the baby is born. Choosing a doctor isn't as easy as it once was, because you must make sure your health insurance covers a particular doctor or, if you don't have insurance, the doctor's fees are affordable.

Start by screening doctors with the some of The Cleveland Clinic questions we listed earlier in this chapter. Add these to your list:

- How often will the doctor see your child per year?
- How crowded is the doctor's calendar? Can you schedule an appointment within a reasonable time?
- Is her office close enough to make office visits convenient?
- How long are the office visits? Are you permitted in the examining room with your child?
- What are the evening and weekend office hours? Is there a 24-hour phone number you can call for advice?
- Where can you take your child in emergency situations or outside of office hours? Will you be able to get to this location quickly? Who will care for your child in these situations?
- What is his philosophy of infant feeding and nutrition?

- How much child-raising guidance does he provide?
- Does the provider want the family to call her with any concern, or only with critical concerns?

Once again, ask people you trust for recommendations, and take a pass if the doc doesn't like the questions.

The American Academy of Pediatrics has an easy-to-use online referral service at aap.org/referral. The AAP also has wonderful parenting guidelines and suggestions online.

Your health insurance provider has a list of participating pediatricians in your area. If the physician you want to use isn't part of your insurance plan's system, push the insurance company to cover visits anyway. The company may allow it, but it usually means more paperwork for you.

Choosing Child Care

At first glance, child care options seem pretty simple. You can bring the baby to a day care center or someone else's home. You can bring someone into your home to care for the baby.

Using a Pro

Day care centers serve larger numbers of children, a feature that has its pros and cons. More kids and more variety of kids give your child the chance for strong social and intellectual development and stimulation as she ages. On the other hand, employees face the challenge of giving sufficient individual attention to each child. She may catch colds more often from the other kids, but may also develop stronger immunities to childhood illness.

The National Association of Child Care Resource and Referral Agencies suggest that you look, listen, count, and ask:

Look to see if the place seems safe, the staff seems to enjoy interacting with and caring for the kids, and toys and learning materials are within a child's reach. Stay around to get a good feel for things—and continue to visit the place you eventually choose.

Listen to hear if the infant area is calm and quiet, so baby can sleep easily. Do the children sound happy and involved? Do the teachers' voices seem cheerful and patient? A place that's too quiet may mean not enough activity. A place that's too noisy may mean there is a lack of control.

Count the number of children and staff members caring for them. Obviously, the fewer the number of children for each adult, the more attention your child will get. A small number of children per adult is most important for babies and younger children.

Ask about the background and experience of all staff and any other adults who will have contact with your child. Find out about the special training each one has and whether the program is accredited. Quality care providers and teachers are happy to answer these questions.

Another person's home can be a good choice, whether it belongs to a relative or a licensed professional. A significant percentage of children are cared for by grandparents or other relatives, and this can develop strong family ties while providing your child with familiar surroundings. However, not all relatives are willing or able to care for small children, so be sure you don't put the relatives or the baby in a tough spot.

A licensed in-home child care provider usually has one or two adults caring for a small number of kids in her own home. Just as in a day care center, the attention and stimulation your baby gets will depend on the provider's philosophy and the ratio of adults to kids.

As with a day care center, be sure to check references and visit the places you're considering.

Bringing It Home

Of course, you can also bring someone into your own home to care for the baby. Relatives can be a good option here, depending on the situation. You can also hire individual child care providers, like a nanny. Check references thoroughly and interview candidates. Start with a trial period, even with relatives. That allows you and the caregiver to judge how capable the provider is and how well your child hits it off with him or her.

The nanny option has regained favor in recent years, but there is work involved for you. Employing a nanny is like owning a company with employees. You have to screen candidates, check references, keep records, perform job reviews, allow vacations, handle payroll taxes, and all the rest. Some parents use a nanny agency, and some seek candidates on their own. Either way, ask lots of questions and be prepared—this is your child we're talking about here!

At-Home Moms and Dads

If you can afford it, the most traditional child care option is mom staying home with the baby. However, some women (my wife included) have a strong need to keep a career or do other outside activities to help retain an identity separate from the baby.

The number of stay-at-home fathers is growing steadily due to a number of factors. Some men do it because they instinctively feel well suited and/or called to the task. Some do it because they've been laid off. A dad may stay home because his partner has the higher salary, and his income wouldn't cover the cost of professional day care.

Many at-home dads (a.k.a. AHDs) re-enter the paid workforce after their children enter school. Others remain primary parent for years beyond. Longitudinal research by Yale psychiatrist Kyle Pruitt, MD and others indicates that at-home dads have stronger bonds with their children than other fathers (a common sense example of how quantity facilitates quality). In addition, the children seem to have more confidence and a stronger sense of self. Studies also suggest that, when compared to families who use professional day care, working mothers are more involved in their children's lives when the father stays at home.

As writer and at-home dad Buzz McClain says, "You can't get laid off from this job."

Family and Friends

You will need the help of relatives and friends in the weeks, months, and years ahead. Much of the time, they're happy to help. However, you retain full permission to be both gracious and judicious in accepting the help.

I had trouble getting along with my mother-in-law, and so dreaded her visit when our twins were about three months old. Man, was I in for a surprise. Phyllis was eager, affectionate, and silly with the girls. She made us sleep in while she did nighttime feedings. She had a blast and was very good at this nurturing stuff. I'd seldom seen these qualities in her before. It was like she was a different person. Even more amazing—the same thing happened to my reserved father-in-law when he visited a month later.

This taught me an important lesson. You don't always see all of who a person is and what she has to offer before a certain set of circumstances (like having a grandchild) comes along. That set of circumstances can transform someone into a better person. So, don't be too quick to judge or rule out how a relative or friend can help you.

At the same time, you need to be clear about when, where, and how you want help. You and your partner are the primary parents, and you have to figure out how to raise this child (in the end, grandparents go home).

So, welcome the wisdom and experience of your parents and other people who raised kids. But don't let them dictate what you do.

In addition, keep an eye out for attitudes or behaviors (from your family as well as hers) that reinforce the idea that you have a secondary role in raising this child. Chances are good that your folks and your in-laws mean well, but in their generation, active father involvement wasn't as common as today. Your relatives have a lot of wisdom to offer, but you and your partner have the ultimate responsibility—and opportunity!—to raise this child in your own way.

You're allowed to say lovingly and firmly, "Mom and dad, I want your help and support. However, we're the ones who have to learn how to raise the baby, so you have to let us make those decisions for ourselves. We even want you to let us learn from our mistakes."

Psst. Mom, Over Here

This is the only part of this book that mom has to read. So, put the book down for a minute, and go ask your partner to look over this brief lesson on culture, gender, and parenting.

No, I'm not kidding; go get her now. I'll wait. This is an *Idiot's Guide*, so it isn't going anywhere without you telling it to.

Are you both back now? Okay, here's what you both need to know:

Through both subtle and blatant attitudes, most of us get into the habit of seeing child-rearing as a mother's job. Mom usually does the feeding, schedules the sitter, instructs dad, grandparents, and babysitters on the proper way to change diapers, and is the person of last resort when the baby won't stop crying. Dad defers because that's what he's supposed to do; he's no expert—and who actually enjoys dirty diapers?

Mom often becomes the gatekeeper of child rearing—even in families fully committed to equally shared parenting. This is not the best pattern for the health and well-being of baby, dad, or mom.

The Invisible Gatekeeper

One thing is absolutely clear: mothers and fathers don't fall into gatekeeping habits in order to get back at each other, win a power struggle, or because one parent loves the baby more than the other one. We adopt these habits because we grew up in a world that taught us to divvy up parenting responsibilities by gender.

Mom takes on the gatekeeper role (and fathers forfeit it) unconsciously and with the best intentions. The arrangement may seem logical.

Think about it: how much babysitting do teenage boys usually do? Not much; we don't expect—and often we don't want—boys to care for kids. So, dad often has less experience than mom with feeding, burping, and rocking a baby to sleep. But a Mother-Knows-Best model only looks logical if you accept some pretty screwy cultural notions about gender roles in society.

Sharing the Load

One screwy notion is that child rearing is exclusively women's work. Close behind is the notion that men don't (and/or don't know how to) "do" child-rearing. Men are supposed to bring in the money and look proudly upon the kiddies from afar.

Don't get me wrong; child rearing is women's work. But it's also men's work. The default cultural standards leave dad out. That makes more work for mom. It also tends to make mom and child hungry for more of dad, and distances dad from experiences and relationships that are really good for him (not to mention the rest of the family). Need proof? Look back at the "Dose of Daddy Data" section of Chapter 1.

It takes work, courage, and open communication to defy widespread conventions that lessen expectations and opportunities for dad to get in the game of child-rearing. Nevertheless, it is worth the effort.

Both of you will make mistakes. That's okay and totally normal. You will solve problems differently from one another—and the problem will still be solved. Just because parent A does something opposite from parent B, that doesn't necessarily mean either way is wrong. Share the work and share the wonder! Enjoy your ride together as parents.

The Least You Need to Know

- Be involved in choosing and working with doctors and other professionals.
- Take your time when selecting caregivers for your child, and visit the home or facility more than once before making a final decision.
- You can welcome and limit help from family and friends.
- Sharing the parenting is worth the work.

Exhibition Games

In This Chapter

- Learning from pregnancy
- Coaching prep for labor and delivery
- Planning the birth day
- Getting your own life in shape

Okay, now we're getting down to launch time. You have a few more weeks or days until momma goes into labor and it feels like all hell breaks loose.

This is actually a window of opportunity. You can do some special and fun things, even though she's now waddling through the world.

Nature will also be giving you your final preparation for becoming the father of a newborn. The evidence is right in front of you.

The Great Mimic

Your partner is irritable, huge, and achy. Nothing seems to make her comfortable. She can't help getting up in the middle of the night—waking you up, too—to pee every hour, or more. Her eating and sleeping schedule gets completely out of whack.

Other times, your partner is energized, with sparkling eyes and glowing skin. The feeling that she can conquer the world is so contagious that you feel that way, too. The two of you find new ways of snuggling, giving each other a deeper level of affection and comfort than you ever thought possible. You discover new and exciting qualities in each other almost daily.

Now, stop and think about what an infant spends time doing. Getting irritated, with nothing more than a variation in crying to tell you why. Gurgling and giggling when she lays eyes on you. Peeing (and pooping) over and over and over. Responding instantly to the feel and smell of your skin and hair, relaxing every muscle in his body. Getting up in the middle of the night, every night. Eating on a schedule that defies any order and logic.

Sleeping. Waking up. Sleeping. Waking up.

See a pattern here? The ways in which your partner's pregnancy affects your life mimic the ways that your newborn baby will affect your life. Especially during the pregnancy's final weeks.

Knowing how pregnancy mimics parenting a newborn, you might just panic, or you might want to throw up your hands and jump overboard. Take a deep breath. In fact, your expectant father days help get your parenting sea legs under you.

D'ya Hear About the Baby with Four Ears?

People say amazingly dumb things to expecting parents. Here are some of my favorites:

- Are you sure you're the father?
- I didn't put on that much weight when I was pregnant.
- My sister hadn't felt a kick yet either, and hers was stillborn.
- She's pregnant? Isn't it about time you finally get a decent job?

This is the time for you to put on your "father as protector" gear. If your partner or you get upset when the next door neighbor starts sharing awful stories from her 36-hour delivery or 36-month adoption process, politely and firmly tell the neighbor to stop.

Listen to a veteran dad:

"When we told a good friend that we were pregnant, she immediately told us horror stories from her relatives and even people she'd met on a plane. I had enough. I said, 'We need to change the subject now.' Later on in our pregnancy, some of that friend's experiences did help us. But by setting some limits, I think we helped her be more sensitive in how she approached us, and we knew more about what information and support we needed."

If someone is just plain rude and obnoxious, don't be afraid to promptly don your shining armor, take your partner's hand, and walk away.

On the other hand, most people say wonderful, supportive things to expectant parents. So be sure to stick around that part, too; take off your armor, and bask in the excitement!

One Last R&R

By now, you know that your baby's arrival will lead to radical change in your life and relationships. Okay, as a veteran dad, I'm required to admit that you don't really know much of this until delivery day comes, but you have some idea.

If your partner's pregnancy is going well and you both have time off available, consider taking a vacation during this final stretch. It's wise to finish your trip at least a month before the due date, so you don't invite trouble. Absolutely get her doctor's okay before setting off.

 DAD WORDS

My favorite part of the pregnancy was rubbing her tummy and feeling the hits and kicks when the baby was active. I also LOVED parading my pregnant wife around because I really thought she was so beautiful and epitomized the essence of womanhood.

—Andy

The goal here is relaxed, special alone time for you and her. Climbing a mountain or conquering the nearest Thrill-o-rama amusement park, not so much. With every week, your partner has more work in moving herself around, dealing with backaches, and needing to pee as baby crushes mommy's bladder. Keeping this in mind will improve the odds of actually enjoying your vacation!

It may not be smart to surprise your highly hormonal honey with a trip of your own design. You know your situation best, of course, but it's probably best to plan your getaway together.

Keep it low key, cherish the one-on-one time, and embrace the thrills of becoming new parents. You're about to get a long hiatus from "just the two of us" trips, and this one can be very special.

Coaching the Quarterback

"Okay, now Honeybunch; the three-nurse blitz is on, the OB is running a hook-'n-go, so deliver that baby far enough downfield to clear the heart monitor!"

By this point, you should've attended enough childbirth education classes to know your partner isn't looking for this kind of coaching on Game Day.

Father participation in these classes is normal nowadays—in part because they're actually quite enjoyable. You learn things about the labor and delivery process, and you master some practical ways to be helpful.

So, be consistent about going and conscientious about doing your homework.

Slackers tend to leave their partners feeling abandoned, and they pay a price; remember, this is an intensely hormonal woman you're dealing with!

Coaching Styles

The idea of childbirth classes is simple: to give you some basic info and answer your questions. You'll watch some films, talk about what happens at the hospital, find out what to expect during a C-section, and other things. You'll also learn breathing and relaxation techniques that both of you can use during labor and delivery.

You can continue using these techniques for years to come when in the dentist's chair, giving blood, or watching your kid's first varsity pole vault.

Your OB/GYN, hospital, midwife, and local American Red Cross chapter can recommend classes nearby. Over the years, experts have developed slightly different methods, but the reputable ones all emphasize two important facts:

- Childbirth is a natural process, not a disease to be cured. (We did it for years before classes came along.)
- A father is his partner's most crucial resource in pregnancy, labor, and delivery.

Make sure you know who is sponsoring the classes, that the instructor is certified, and that you know the dates, times, and locations of each class.

Nearly every hospital and birthing center offers childbirth classes, and they often have sliding fee scales. There really isn't anything else worth more investment of your time and money. So show up!

Lamaze is the most common approach in North America. Created by (spoiler alert) Dr. Ferdinand Lamaze in the 1950s, this method teaches relaxation, external focus, and breathing. Lamaze observed Russian women using Pavlovian conditioning to control breathing and relaxation to give birth without anesthetics. (Yes, this is the same dog-trainer/psychologist Pavlov you studied in Psych 101.)

The father is central to the Lamaze method. Dad coaches and does breathing exercises with mom during the pregnancy (for practice) and during labor and delivery.

Lamaze encourages the mother to focus on comfort and move around during labor. You can learn more and find a nearby class at lamaze.org, the online home of Lamaze International.

The Bradley Method emphasizes healthy nutrition and avoidance of alcohol, drugs, tobacco and the like during pregnancy. It's named for Kansan obstetrician Robert Bradley, who lobbied in the 1940s to get husbands into the delivery room (earning major dad brownie points).

Bradley also relies on breathing and relaxation, but encourages the mother's focus to be internal, rather than external. Mom learns how to close her eyes and get in tune with what's happening inside her body, thereby helping the process to go smoothly, naturally, and with less pain (in theory). Of course, the dad is key to coaching mom through this process and keeping her focused. Learn more at bradleybirth.com.

Leboyer methods aim to reduce baby's stress and shock as he passes from womb to the cold, hard world. Research hasn't proven with finality that baby is calmer or more alert if Mother (and Father) are partially submerged in a specially designed warm tub during delivery. But the dimmed lights and quiet surroundings can reduce parental stress and discomfort.

Leboyer advocates placing the baby on mom's abdomen or at her breast for some time before cutting the umbilical cord—standard practice now for healthy newborns at many hospitals and birthing centers. Some hospitals have installed birthing pools; make sure yours has the expertise to use one correctly. Ask lots of questions if you decide to go this route.

EXTRA POINT

So mom is on complete bed rest at your remote Nebraska ranch, or there's another reason you and/or she can't get to childbirth classes in person. Google "virtual childbirth class," and you'll find several choices.

Use your concern about your partner's well-being as motivation to help keep a positive focus on doctor visits, healthy eating, and exercise. Recognize how well she's handling all the demands on her time, mind, and body. And then reassure yourself (and her) that she'll be fine.

The Gameday Playsheet

Many expectant parents write up a birth plan that tells doctors, nurses, and others what they want and expect to happen during the pregnancy, labor, and delivery. You list your desires about using anesthesia, getting an episiotomy, who you want in the labor and/or delivery room, and the like. Work on the plan with your OB/GYN, because it's really an agreement between you and her about your vision for the birth.

A birth plan gives you a place in planning and helps you and mom be explicit about your wishes with each other and with the professionals. Of course, there's no guarantee that a breech baby won't poke a big hole in your quiet, incense-laden scenario; first priority is always the safety and health of baby and mother.

However, a birth plan is worth the effort. It is especially helpful if you go into labor while your OB/GYN is out of town or off duty. You can give the birth plan to the doctor who does attend you, and he'll have a concrete guide to your approach. Deliver a complete copy to your OB/GYN and the hospital or birthing center—then ask them to attach it to your partner's medical record. Make sure you have a copy, too, and then bring it with you when your partner goes into labor. You'll find birth plan tools and samples online.

> **HEADS UP**
>
> Any childbirth that produces a living child and mother is a natural childbirth. Don't let anyone tell you that you "failed" if you had a caesarean delivery or choose to have painkillers administered during labor. You, your partner, and your OB/GYN get to make the call—not your neighbors, family, self-help books, or childbirth instructors.

You can also save time and headache on delivery day by visiting the hospital ahead of time to fill out admission forms. They'll gather info about you two, your insurance, your doctor, and so on. That means less paperwork in the chaos of arriving with your partner in labor. And it's much easier than filing your taxes.

I Have Needs, Too, Ya Know

The transformation from man to father is big, no matter how excited you are by the prospect. You have tons of questions, no previous experience, and intense desires to protect your baby and your partner.

Expecting a baby is stressful for mom and dad both. The antidote for stress is to actively and consciously care for your body and your spirit.

Real Men Don't Get Stressed

Consider the title of this little section like a true/false quiz. The correct answer is … false. Men stress out for one simple reason: we are human, and stress is a natural human occurrence.

Unfortunately, we tend to respond to stress by putting on what my friend Jackson Katz calls our "Tough Guise." We believe we can't ask for help or let any vulnerability show.

Think about pro athletes who have long careers. Their longevity is usually tied to how coachable they make themselves. When they develop a hitch in their swing or struggle with the cover-two, they admit it—and ask trusted coaches and peers for help. A little coaching and guidance will improve your fathering game no matter how old your child is. In fathering, vulnerability is the opposite of weakness. Vulnerability is the open door through which we get better at the job and bond with our children, giving us the strongest human connections we may ever have.

A great way to relieve stress and keep your spirits up is to communicate, communicate, communicate (have I mentioned that before?) with your partner, family, friends, and the health care pros. Let them know what you need, what you're thinking, and what you're feeling. Yes, even what you're feeling!

EXTRA POINT

Regular doses of exhilaration will give you energy and adrenaline to carry you through the stresses of expecting, labor, delivery, and the rest of your child's life!

Be sure to tune in to the signs of stress in your partner, too. Human nature seems to dictate that other people notice our stress before we do ourselves. So be considerate and supportive when she is wigged out.

This may require prudent use of the strategic white lie, especially during labor. No, you shouldn't pretend that green is blue (some of us never pretend; we're color blind and can't tell the difference), or stifle important thoughts and feelings. But there are occasions when you help your cause—and ease your stress—by delivering a "Yes, dear" or a "No, you look fabulous" even if that's not your genuine sentiment at the moment.

The key word is *strategic*. Less can be more in a loving relationship. If you seldom get yourself into jams where you need a white lie on a regular basis, then you don't develop bad habits. With discretion, one considerate fib can help both of you feel better.

Of course, action is often better than words alone. You can take many concrete steps to reduce stress for the both of you. Increase your housekeeping and laundry output. Don't worry if you're inexperienced—the detergent bottles have instructions simple enough for first-time users to follow.

Provide her with comfort in her favorite forms. Rub her feet, read to her, make her a mixed tape of her favorite songs, or sing to her. Massage her neck and shoulders (check with her physician before attempting full-body massage). Prepare her favorite comfort foods; you can Google every recipe from mac-and-cheese to mushroom-stuffed beef tenderloin. And don't forget the wonderful world of take-out!

Ignore the Score

We love sports, statistics, and knowing the score. We focus a lot on winners and losers in our culture and society. But that's a bad idea in fathering.

Keeping score is useless in parenting. In fact, it's usually harmful.

The life of a family has nothing in common with the Super Bowl, World Series, or zero-sum accounting ... even on those days when you feel like life is clipping you every down while the ref looks the other way. No one will win if you and your partner start competing for the title of "most stressed," "most diapers changed," or "most put-upon."

The parenting games lasts exponentially longer than a soccer game—or even a cricket test match! When your child grows up, he won't use a spreadsheet or scorecard to judge how you did as a father. Instead, he'll care about how you and your partner nurtured, supported, and challenged him. He'll consider you a winner if you listen to him, take him seriously, and help him know how much he can contribute to the world.

Of course, you're still human, so you may sometimes find yourself slipping into "I do/hurt/work/worry more than you" mode from time to time. Whenever you feel yourself going there, remember that keeping score in families produces no winners. It only generates hurt and resentment.

READING THE SIGNS

Open communication releases the pressure valves and makes it easier to tune in to the good, exciting, and energizing things happening in your fathering arena.

Speaking of resentment, throw it out of your dad toolbox, and don't let it back in. You will be tempted at times to feel resentful; for example, when she gets all the attention and you seem ignored. But choosing resentment as a tool to respond is bound to jam your gears.

The reason is simple. Resentment eats away at the resentor long before it impacts the resentee (if it ever does). When you resent something that's happening, the first person you undermine is yourself. As many wise men have said: resentment is like you taking poison and expecting the other guy to die.

Plus, resentment never solves the problem, making it a terribly lousy tool. Change comes from action and constructive attitudes. If a new (or veteran) dad is resentful, he can expect nothing but trouble. So don't go there.

I Don't Need a Doctor to Be Healthy

This pregnancy is bringing major changes to your life and your body. Some of the changes are obvious, and others will take some time (maybe years) to understand.

You might even have to make radical modifications in your own behavior, especially when it comes to your health.

Research from the Centers for Disease Control and Prevention (CDC) finds that men are 80 percent less likely than women to use a regular source of health care. Translation: we don't go to the doctor unless we think we are really sick. Outcome: we don't get the benefits of preventive care to reduce the odds of getting sick in the first place.

You have just as much incentive to take care of your body as your partner does. The better health you're in, the more stamina and resources you give your partner during pregnancy—not to mention your partner and your kids for the rest of your life. Now hear this: your child really does want you around for as long as possible.

Be sure to exercise. You may not get to the gym or play softball as often as you did before, but don't drop out completely. Exercise definitely helps reduce stress and anxiety—both common features of Daddydom. Plus, exercise helps you stay in touch with your body.

It may seem paradoxical, but staying attuned to your body can deepen your connection to your partner and children. For example, pregnancy forces your partner to be conscious of how her body is working. If you do the same with your body, you join in a sharing, empathetic frame of mind with her.

Garbage In, Garbage Out

Another must is eating well and ingesting wisely. If you haven't already, start to eat a balanced and healthy diet (and ditch toxic chemicals like nicotine). Eating healthy will give you the energy and clear-headedness to be more useful to your partner and kids.

If your partner has to observe special nutritional guidelines during pregnancy, you follow them too. Only a saint doesn't resent it when her partner pigs out on a cheesesteak, fries, and malt across the table from her salad, fruit, and Emetrol. Being rude at mealtime leaves a bad taste in her mouth. Go along with her meal plan. If you absolutely must have a banana split, get it when you're by yourself.

DAD WORDS

The only way to keep your health is to eat what you don't want, drink what you don't like, and do what you druther not.

—Mark Twain

Smoking, alcohol, and illicit drugs are poison to your baby, before and after birth. It's much harder for a pregnant woman to stop using these chemicals if her partner keeps on using them (besides which, it's not fair to her). So stop now.

Every state and most insurance companies have smoking cessation programs—these greatly improve the odds of kicking an addictive habit that will always endanger your child. Use them. Kids living with secondhand smoke are far more likely to get asthma.

If you or your partner have difficulty giving up alcohol or other drugs when the stakes are this high, you may need a hand. Millions of people misuse alcohol and/or other drugs, so you're not alone if you develop a problem. Fortunately, millions of people recover with the right help. Look in the Yellow Pages under alcohol or drug treatment. Or, access these organizations for free information:

- National Organization on Fetal Alcohol Syndrome at www.nofas.org
- National Institute on Alcohol Abuse and Alcoholism at niaaa.nih.gov
- Substance Abuse & Mental Health Services Administration at samhsa.gov
- Alcoholics Anonymous at aa.org
- Narcotics Anonymous at na.org

Addiction wrecks families, so there's every reason in the world to act now if you have trouble with smoking, alcohol, or drugs. Your kids will thank you for it, and you'll thank yourself, since your life will be a lot healthier and happier.

Extreme Makeover: Home Edition

When I was a kid, my sisters cooked and cleaned, while I mowed the lawn and emptied the garbage. One day, my sister asked why I had once-a-week chores, but she had to cook or wash clothes and dishes every day. My mom replied, "He'll learn to clean and cook in the Army." Even I had to admit her answer was weak.

Well, dad, if you haven't learned to cook, clean, and launder, now is the time to start. You and your partner will have your hands full with a new baby, so you're much better off if both of you can handle the most essential tasks around the house (like preparing food). Plus, one infant will generate more than twice as many dirty clothes as the two of you can produce. (However, please don't try competing with baby on this one.)

The expectant months are an ideal time to pick up and/or refine your home front skills. You have time to experiment with recipes and cooking methods that suit your style, schedule, and personality. You have time to learn which of your partner's delicates can't go in the dryer, and how to iron your own shirts (tip: switch to permanent press; ironing is way less fun than playing with the baby—or sleeping).

For goodness sake, don't get hung up in the notion that cooking and cleaning are beneath a man. Cooking, cleaning, burping, changing diapers, earning money, comforting tears—it's all parents' work. Only a fool divvies up those necessary tasks by arbitrary (and silly) concepts of gender roles. As if those guys on KP and latrine duty in the Army aren't manly?

 DAD WORDS

Watching your husband become a father is really sexy and wonderful.
—Cindy Crawford

Want a simple, effective approach? Do half the work, all the time, 24 hours a day, 7 days a week, 52 weeks a year. Divide up the duties with your partner based on interest, skill, and/or necessity. You may hate doing laundry and she may hate cleaning the bathroom. So, she does most of the laundry and you clean the bathroom. If you both hate the same thing, flip a coin.

Change half the diapers. Give half the baths. Do half the feedings—if the baby isn't breastfeeding, of course. Do half the nighttime rocking chair/baby walking duty. Always be a parent, never a babysitter.

Your infant's arrival will bring lots of clutter, messes, and virtually no time to clean. And that may not change for a long time; I once attended a high school grad party where parts of the house clearly hadn't been cleaned since the graduate was born.

You can do everyone a huge favor by giving your home a thorough cleaning before the baby is born. Start with a clean slate and you'll reduce tension in those first weeks of infant care.

If you need guidance, ask for it—but don't let your partner do the work. Her body is on overtime already.

The Least You Need to Know

- Pregnancy prepares your schedule for parenting.
- Don't let other people determine how you experience life changes.
- You are the first and best resource for your partner during pregnancy, labor, and beyond.
- Take care of yourself; your child and partner need you.

Opening Day

2

Your partner's pregnancy is coming to an end. You get the call to leave the bullpen of theoretical dads for your trip onto the playing field of hands-on fathering.

Understatement alert: Your child's birth day and the following days are full and intense. So, this part of the book dedicates major attention to this key period. You find practical tips on getting to the hospital safely, enjoying and surviving your time there, and then getting into a good routine when you bring baby back home.

Fair warning: Caring for an infant—ever-repeating rounds of diapering, feeding, burping, washing clothes, making food, bathing, getting her to sleep, trying to sleep yourself, doing all of this over again—will take huge chunks of your days and nights. Sometimes it will feel like drudgery. Other times it will be great fun, especially when you notice your baby growing or catch her personality in the sparkle of her eyes and the rhythm of her gurgles.

Welcome to a wild and wonderful ride!

Ready, Set, Go!

In This Chapter

- Lining up your logistics
- Recognizing the labor signs
- Supporting your partner
- Getting to the hospital

A lot of things happen during labor and delivery, including some events you can't anticipate ahead of time. Your job: keep your focus centered on your partner, and then on her and the baby. Luckily, you have many months to line up the logistics that make smoother sailing for your partner, your baby, and you.

This chapter tells you how to get ready for the trip to the hospital and how to know when it's time to go there. Fortunately, between birthing classes and the tips I give you here, you can be at your best with all your resources lined up and ready to use.

Birthday Plans

When you and your partner decide it's time to go to the hospital, you'll be operating on adrenaline, euphoria, and panic. So, do your clear thinking ahead of time. Then, when you're called to action, you can just grab your gear and run.

Pre-Flight Screening

By now, you know what hospital or birthing center you'll use for the birth. Make absolutely sure you know how to get there! In the weeks before your due date, try driving to the hospital at different times of day. This gives you a sense of the traffic flow, how much time to allow at rush hour vs. 2 A.M., and ideas for alternative routes if an accident stops traffic.

Find out if there will be construction along your route and the roads that will get you there fastest if a blizzard or thunderstorm hit (hint from a longtime Minnesotan: streets on bus routes usually get plowed first).

At home, make sure the phone number for your OB/GYN and the hospital are prominently displayed, so you won't forget where they are under pressure, and be sure to add them to your contacts in your cellphones. From month eight on, make sure you keep your gas tank full, battery charged, and the car otherwise ready to go. Install the child safety seat in the backseat, so you don't have to remember it after the baby is born. And make sure you know where to find a set of car keys.

EXTRA POINT

Don't tear the house apart looking for the car keys when labor comes. Make at least three extra keys now. Put one inside your wallet and one in your partner's purse. Hang one by the door you open to leave the house and get in the car. If you have a back-up driver, make sure he or she has a key, too.

Recruit someone who lives nearby as a backup driver. A woman in labor should not drive! Make sure your backup has a car (or can easily access and drive yours) and will be available when you're not. Don't pick someone who works the same shift you do or who lives too far away.

If you plan to use public transportation, travel the route weeks ahead of time. Do it at different times of day, so you get a sense of how long it will take. Have a backup plan in case your partner goes into labor at night after the busses stop running. Treat your fare the same way a driver treats his car keys. Put an envelope by your front door with exact change or a fare card for the transit, and/or enough cash to pay a cabby.

If you don't have a car, a taxi is your best option. Call the cab company a few weeks before your due date and find out how fast they can get to you at different times of day, and whether it'll take longer on a weekend. If the time comes, and none of these options will work, call an ambulance.

Birthday Bag for Three, Please

In the movies, tanks, planes, and UFOs roar endlessly into action. No movies revolve around the people putting fuel and ammo into the transports. However, strategic commanders will tell you that the side with better logistical support usually wins.

Remember this as you prepare to be at the hospital for a day and perhaps more. The hospital has the basic tools for labor and delivery, but any other essentials in stock ($5 toothbrushes) will quickly drain your wallet.

Get a good size bag or mid-size suitcase, fill it up with gear, and have it ready by the door you'll run through on your way to the hospital. The bag should include supplies for your partner, the baby, and even for you!

Don't go overboard—you want to fit everything in one bag that you can easily carry with one hand, because your first priority is keeping track of your partner (and you may be schlepping the bag all over the hospital).

For your partner, start with the following, then ask her what else she wants to bring—keeping comfort as priority one:

- Personal toiletries—toothbrush, toothpaste, and hair and skin care items.
- Eyeglasses or contacts and supplies. Bring an extra pair just in case.
- Night gowns for one or two nights (her own will probably feel better than what the hospital provides) and a robe.
- Slippers and warm socks.

- Cotton underwear (three or four pairs) and nursing bras.
- Heavy flow menstrual pads. She'll want these for vaginal discharge after the birth.
- Phone numbers and emails for people you'll want to share your news with.
- A book or magazines to help pass the "hurry up and wait" time inevitable at many institutions.
- Comfortable clothes (and shoes) to go home in.
- Camera, camcorder, or tape recorder and charger(s).
- Digital media device or personal CD player with one or two albums to soothe her, and one or two to energize her.
- A focal point. Some childbirth classes encourage mom to focus on an external object while breathing through labor. My wife and I brought a big stuffed orange Pooh bear. My wife ended up not using him, but I hugged Pooh when the stress got high (and still have the ratty bugger 30+ years later).

EXTRA POINT

Hospitals can be chaotic, so don't bring valuable jewelry, credit cards, large amounts of cash, or fragile items. If your partner wants some comforting reminder of home, bring a teddy bear, not a precious porcelain knickknack.

Your newborn will get some initial baby supplies, like diapers, from the hospital. Many hospitals send you home with a goodie bag of free baby products donated by manufacturers to win your brand loyalty. But your new baby still needs some items from home.

Try leaning down to your partner's belly and asking what your baby wants. If you don't get an answer, you have to choose. (Don't bring him candy bars yet, okay?) Here's where to start:

- Undershirts.
- Socks (don't bring shoes—a baby shouldn't wear shoes until she can walk; they're bad for her feet).
- Receiving blankets—at least three. (I don't think you get a shipping blanket until you ship the kid off to camp.)

- Clothes to go home in. A simple sleeper outfit is best. Include a hat, even if the weather is warm. If it's cold, bring a baby sweater or snowsuit.

- Infant car seat. Remember, they won't let you take the baby home without one. Don't try and fit this in the bag! (Leave it in the car until you need it.)

You, too will also need some things, so be sure your birthday bag includes these items:

- Personal toiletries. Even if you don't spend the night in the hospital, your partner may insist that you brush your teeth.

- Your medications. Please don't pass out during labor because your insulin is home in the bathroom.

- Clothes to sleep in. If you stay over, hospital rooms are not as private as bedrooms; wear a sweat suit or something similar for sleeping.

- A change of clothes (including underwear and socks).

- "Low odor" snacks like granola, dried fruit, nuts, and a Milky Way Midnight bar. (Dark chocolate is an antioxidant—at least, that's my excuse.) Your partner can't eat during labor, but your energy level must remain high. She may, however, be hypersensitive to smells and gag if she finds garlic on your breath as you whisper encouragement in her ear. Stick to simple, high-energy foods that won't smell in the bag or in your mouth.

- A bathing suit. Father expert Armin Brott (mrdad. com) wisely suggests swimming apparel. If the hospital encourages mom to take a shower to relax during labor, a swimsuit lets you join her without scandalizing the staff. You'll also need one if you're using a birthing tub.

- Cellphone and charger. Warning: many hospitals ban cellphones because they may interfere with equipment. Check with your facility and substitute a phone calling card if you must.

- A form for the baby to sign, legally obligating her to support you in your retirement. (Just kidding.)

If you do bring any extras, keep them simple and make sure they fit in one bag. There are a lot more important things to keep track of than CDs and socks. And don't even think about going shopping while she's in labor.

In the end, all the hospital really needs for a successful birth is the mother, you, and the baby. Everything else is optional. So, if she goes into labor at your parents' house, don't go home for your supply bag—get her to the hospital!

Signs of the Time

As the expectant months wind down, the most pressing question for most couples is "When do we go to the hospital?" Believe it or not, most first-time parents know when to go. How can you know if you're rookies? Nature has her ways.

Also, between childbirth classes and this book, you and your partner should be well tuned in to each other by now. You can pick up on tangible and intangible cues from your partner, which indicate that this is the real deal, even if she isn't so sure.

My wife's cervix started dilating a month before her due date, so the doctor ordered complete bed rest (for her, not me). The following Friday morning, she said she thought maybe her water had broken, but that she didn't think we needed to go to the hospital because she didn't feel any strong contractions.

I said, "Are you crazy? I think we should go right away if your water broke." She said no, I said yes; we played verbal tennis for a few minutes, as couples do. Finally, I insisted on at least calling the hospital and explaining the situation. The nurse said, "What are you waiting for? Get in here right away!" Our twins were born by 7:30 that night.

HEADS UP

Even if you get to the hospital "too soon" and they send you home, don't be frustrated or embarrassed. View it as a practice run and remember: going early is better than waiting too long. Meanwhile, stay tuned; your labor day is coming one way or another.

"False" Labor

Starting as early as week 20 of her pregnancy, your partner may feel Braxton Hicks contractions, named for British gynecologist John Braxton Hicks, who first described them in 1872. But, as mothering author Janine DeBaise writes, "This was sort of like Columbus discovering America. Some people already knew it was there."

Braxton Hicks contractions are like wind sprints for your partner's uterus, warming up its muscles for labor contractions and softening up the cervix. Here are some of their key characteristics:

- Irregular in intensity
- Infrequent
- Don't follow a rhythm
- Unpredictable
- More uncomfortable than painful
- Taper off and then disappear altogether

"False labor" lasts from 30 seconds to 2 minutes and can be stimulated by dehydration or exercise. Your partner can usually ease any discomfort by taking a warm bath, changing her body position (rest if she's moving, move if she's resting), drinking water, or practicing her breathing. By the way, Braxton Hicks contractions don't hurt the baby at all.

Be especially vigilant if she is a high risk for delivering prematurely. Call the OB/GYN right away if contractions come more than four times in an hour, produce bloody or watery vaginal discharge, generate lower back pain, or develop a regular pattern. These symptoms may mean labor is starting, and you need to respond right away.

Now Appearing on Stage One ...

Labor has what doctors call three "stages," and stage one has three "phases." Why they don't just make it five stages, I don't know. But you go to the hospital near the end of stage one, phase one, so let's take a look at it.

Stage one's three phases are based on the dilation of the cervix:

- **Phase one:** Relatively mild contractions start dilating the cervix to 3 centimeters (out of 10).
- **Phase two:** Cervix dilates up to 7 centimeters, as contractions intensify.
- **Phase three:** The cervix dilates completely to 10 centimeters, beginning the transition to delivery.

(Stage two of labor consists of delivering the baby and stage three consists of delivering the placenta.)

Usually, stage one, phase one is the longest part of labor, sometimes known as early or latent labor. It is normally the least painful and can actually start days before the birth day, in which case your partner may not notice it much. It can also come on suddenly with contractions she can't miss, and then last anywhere from 2 to 24 hours. If you're looking for an ironclad formula and schedule, you won't find it in childbirth.

Her contractions will be what doctors call "mild to moderate" and they generally last less than a minute each. While they may grow more frequent, they haven't yet developed a regular pattern.

In a low-risk pregnancy, most OB/GYNs recommend waiting until the end of phase one or the start of phase two before going to the hospital. So your job during phase one is to keep your partner comfortable, relaxed, and rested. Her toughest challenges are likely to be cramps and back pain. It's normal for her to have a mucousy vaginal discharge laced with blood, as well as diarrhea and/or indigestion. Don't act grossed out—she's in actual pain, and after all, you did this to her!

Help her smooth the transition to phase two. Rub her back and help her move into positions that feel better. Try sitting on the floor up against a wall, and have her sit between your legs as you hold her body almost upright; this relaxes her, and provides the comfort of your embrace. Do breathing exercises together to help her through the discomfort.

READING THE SIGNS

Encourage her to do what feels good, even if it looks silly. Some women find relief by standing and leaning their heads against the wall. Some get down on hands and knees to get the pressure off their spine. These are examples of my daughter's adage: "Gravity is our friend."

If she's hungry, give her light, easy-to-digest foods and fluids. Don't go for a fast-food burger or ice cream; stick to mild soup and toast, which won't make her sick later. If phase one begins during the day, work to normalize what you do. Distract her with a walk, a TV show, or by cooking a meal or folding laundry together.

Keep a sense of humor and a calm, confident attitude. It's a lot easier to chuckle now than later. Keep the tone light and laugh at the absurdity of making a casserole to freeze when you're only hours away from having a baby.

Conventional wisdom says regular intervals of 5 or 10 minutes between contractions signal the start of active (phase two) labor. However, some women never have a consistent, timed rhythm to their intervals. If contractions are longer, stronger, and more frequent than before, call your doctor and/or go to the hospital. If you get there "too early," you won't be the first or last parents to do so, and only the evil nurses will laugh at you (full disclosure: there are no evil nurses).

Keep yourselves rested, because you both need every ounce of reserves later on. Getting all wound up now won't help later. If it's nighttime and you haven't reached phase two, help her get to sleep and stay asleep. Then, you go to sleep, too.

Take charge of remembering details of the contractions. Time the interval between the start of one and the start of the next one. When they get to be fewer than 10 minutes apart, you're closing in on phase two and your trip to the hospital.

HEADS UP

If you have any doubt about whether it's time to go to the hospital, call your OB/GYN or hospital. If your partner's water breaks, head there right away.

Hit the Road, Jack

By the time you've reached phase two of stage one (cervix dilates up to seven centimeters, as contractions intensify), you should be at the hospital. Of course, you have no way of measuring her cervical dilation (as if she'd let you!), so you'll need other clues to know if you're there yet.

Phase two is often called "active labor" because contractions last longer than earlier ones and are markedly more intense. As one doctor says, "If a woman calls me on the phone during a contraction, I can usually tell by the tone of her voice whether she's ready to go to the hospital."

When taking your partner to the hospital, your first task is to do it calmly and safely. Call ahead before you leave, if you can. When you arrive, make sure you (not your partner) fill out any remaining registration and permission forms and field as many questions as you can—so she can focus on her labor. Don't let any red tape waylay you from your first responsibility: being with your partner.

If you have a birthing plan, make sure there's a copy in her medical record, signed by mom and doctor, along with reasons why and when the plan can't be followed (e.g., fetal distress). Have a copy with you at all times to show to the staff and OB/GYNs, especially if your personal OB/GYN isn't available. If the nursing shift changes, have the incoming staff read the plan and make sure they understand your preferences.

Hospital Hijinks

After clearing the admission desk, someone will take you and your partner to your labor or birthing room, with a possible detour to an assessment (or triage) room. Staff will do diagnostic tests on your partner: blood pressure, pulse, urine sample, respiration, taking her temperature, checking her vaginal discharge, and so on. They may set up a fetal monitor and require your partner to change into a hospital gown. Soon after arriving, she will have a vaginal exam, where the OB/GYN checks for cervical dilation and other progress.

Make the labor room as comfortable as possible for your partner and you. Some women want the lights dimmed, mood music, and the door closed to block out distractions. Others want the distraction of hearing what's happening in the hallway, watching TV, and listening to peppy music. Follow her lead, even when her direction does a quick and illogical 180. When a woman is in labor, don't attempt to hold her to anything she said three minutes ago. Or three seconds ago. Go with the flow, man.

DAD WORDS

A baby is God's opinion that life should go on.

—Carl Sandburg

Phase Two

In phase two, there's less time between contractions, so your partner has to concentrate harder on relaxing. She may get annoyed, impatient, and weary about this. Your number one job is to help her through it any way you can.

Because contractions are now longer and more painful, she is turning her attention completely to her body and what's happening to it. She'll have more of the vaginal discharge known as "bloody show," along with aching legs, growing fatigue, and backache.

Some contractions are so intense that she can't even speak during them. She may despair that labor will never end, and 20 seconds later feel elated that labor is progressing so fast. One moment she may cry desperately for your help, and the next she may gruffly inform you that she can do it all by herself. Continue to go with the flow.

If she's using pain relief, such as an epidural, it has to be given before the end of phase two. Ask your OB/GYN for the deadline after which it's too close to delivery for him to administer pain medication.

Phase Three

This last phase of stage one is the transition into stage two: delivering the baby. It can be the shortest phase, but also the toughest, because your partner has been at this for a while now, and wants to get it over with.

Fighting the impulse to "get this over with now!" may be the biggest challenge of phase three. As her cervix reaches full dilation, she will have the seemingly irresistible urge to push the baby out. You must help her hold back until the OB/GYN says it's time to start delivery.

You may have heard stories of women in labor telling their partners:

- I am completely fed up with this and I'm going home.
- How did you get me into this? I'm never letting you touch me again!
- Go away; I'm not talking to you anymore.

These stories are true. It's normal for your partner to feel (and even say) these things. Of course she can't go home, and she will sleep with you again. But her labor-induced feelings and thoughts stem from the pain, fatigue, fear, confusion, and frustration she's experiencing. It's a lot for her to handle. That means it's a lot for you to handle, too.

After the baby arrives, she may also say, "That was the coolest thing ever; I can't wait to do it again!" Logic is not a major element of this life episode.

In Chapter 7, I discuss things you can do and say—and things *not* to do or say—to get you both through this ordeal. First, one more thing about your place in the game.

You're No Bench Player

Health care workers have more experience delivering babies than you do. Sometimes they treat an expectant dad as invisible or in the way. Hospitals are getting a lot better about this, but there are ways to prevent being shunted aside, or deal if a "professional" rolls over you.

Simple and direct etiquette usually smooths relations with physicians and other hospital staff. "When a new health care professional comes into your labor room, introduce yourself," Joy Dorscher, MD, says. "It may seem repetitive if numerous people pass through, but say, 'Hello, I'm so-and-so, and I am the husband (or coach) here.' Most doctors and nurses want to know who you are, and be able to call you by name."

 DAD WORDS

My father carries around the picture of the kid who came with his wallet.
—Rodney Dangerfield

Most OB ward professionals welcome questions, and have experience explaining things in lay language. So, ask (politely) why someone is doing a procedure, and ask if there is more than one option for you to consider. And if a particular staff member isn't interested in answer your questions, don't give up. Find someone else and keep answering until you know what you need to know.

"Be your partner's advocate, but not an obstructionist," Dorscher says. "Speak up, and don't be afraid to say, 'My partner is busy right now, can you explain to me what you're after, or why you're doing what you're doing?'"

"When I give an instruction, like 'go slower as you count your way through this contraction,' I make sure that both parents understand that I'm speaking to both mom and dad. I appreciate it when a dad is direct with his requests, like, 'Is that something I can do instead of you or the nurse?' However, both parents need to understand that if a problem arises, I have to act immediately. That's why they have me there, and I need their immediate cooperation."

The more you stay engaged throughout labor, the more respect you're likely to get from the professionals around you. Your partner has plenty on her mind, so she needs you to advocate and listen for her even if no one (including her) seems to appreciate your effort in the moment.

Remember the point of this whole exercise: baby!

The Least You Need to Know

- Plan ahead for what to do and what to bring.
- You are a key player in labor, delivery, and everything baby.
- Medical staff should help you both, so be sure to stay included in discussions and decisions.
- Give your labor and delivery role everything you've got. Follow your partner's lead, and be her guide.

Can I Survive This Birth?

7

In This Chapter

- Thinking before speaking
- Passing through labor's stages
- Pop goes the baby!
- Sharing the news

A friend says he felt like an ape and a rhino during his wife's labor. "I bounced around like an ape, being silly to distract her. And I needed a rhino's skin to deflect all the things she said to—and about—me. I knew she didn't really mean them, but they were hard to hear."

You are your partner's key ally during labor and delivery, no matter how she treats you during a contraction. Now that the big day has arrived, you must pull out all that you've learned, combine it with the instincts nature gives you, and go the distance.

You may run into some hurdles along the way, but you can handle them.

What to Say and Stifle

Regardless of what happens during labor, you need to present your partner with an upbeat, comforting, encouraging face. This isn't the place to work out long-standing issues in your relationship, even if she chooses this moment to throw them in your goofy, grinning face. Remember that it takes two people to have an argument. If you don't participate, she'll eventually move on to her next contraction or distraction.

Don't rise to the bait if your partner says things that would hurt your feelings if spoken over breakfast or dinner. She's in pain and turmoil, so there's no point in discussing it. It's also beside the point, which is delivering the baby.

HEADS UP

When someone is hurting, it's natural to say, "I know how you feel." Although this phrase is well-intentioned, stifle it during labor. Erase it from your memory bank. Say it and risk hearing: "Bulls—t! You're a man and, damn it, you'll never know how this feels!" She's right; you don't (and it is worse than a toothache or kidney stone).

A few clueless guys corrode our labor day cred with dopey and thoughtless comments. Don't add to the problem with winners like these:

- I'm putting a video of that last pelvic exam up on Facebook.
- The big game just went into overtime; can you hold off until it's over?
- Nothing's happened for a while, so I'm going home to get some sleep. Call me when you go into labor.

Labor doesn't operate predictably. It can go quickly or very slowly. Labor can require intense concentration for a relatively brief period. Or it can have long, boring stretches, followed by—or interspersed with—intense concentration periods. If this is your partner's first baby, there's a higher chance that labor will be longer. The first birth tends to loosen up a woman's innards, speeding the process next time around.

Whether you're in the slow or fast lane, your partner is feeling everything intently. Boring to you may feel boring and scary to her as she wonders about what's next. Has her body ever gone through anything this intense before?

Keep that in mind as you choose your words and attitudes. If you feel boredom creeping on, remind yourself that these are the last quiet moments you'll have together for a long time. Enjoy them, even if she doesn't reciprocate with the same enthusiasm.

Do everything you can to plug your piehole before blurting out "I'm bored," "This is gross," or "Why don't you just get comfortable?"

Keep your eye on the big picture: this is a major and miraculous moment in both of your lives. Cherish it and stifle the urge to complain about minor irritations.

Labor 1.2 and Its Upgrade, 1.3

Now that stage one, phase one is over (see Chapter 6 for details on the stages and phases of labor and delivery), you both should be in the hospital. She will be encountering intense pain—with you as her guide and companion. (If you decide to identify as Yoda, keep it to yourself.) Help her relax and conserve energy. Breathe along through each contraction, if she wants you to—breathing along with her might make her tense or keep her from concentrating. But always remember that she can quickly change her mind, and stand ready to respond. Logic has little place here and now.

What to Do in Phase Two

Acknowledge her pain. Instead of saying "I know how you feel," try, "I know it hurts, honey, and I know you can make it through. You're doing great." Remember that she hurts even if she doesn't say anything; tell her that she doesn't have to be stoic for you.

Handle only one contraction at a time. Don't worry about the next one in the middle of this one. Don't criticize her or how she's doing things. Act the way you would want her to act if she was helping you through hours of intense pain. Encourage and reassure her. If encouraging words make her tense, then encourage and reassure silently with your eyes and touch.

Work with her to make her comfortable. If the hospital allows her to take a walk or a shower, and she thinks it'll help, go along with her.

Your relaxing and comforting touch can go a long way. Some doctors say that massaging her back while she's sitting up may speed labor along. She may want you to rub her feet all the way through labor, or she may make you switch spots every five minutes. The massage may feel great one minute and drive her crazy the next. Do what she wants. If anything you do makes her anxious, try something else.

Be her ice chip man. Sucking on ice chips or frozen juice pops is distracting and keeps her hydrated. Have ice chips ready at all times and put them lovingly in her mouth whenever she wants. (The hospital will have a supply.) At the other end, make sure she has warm socks if her feet are cold.

She may also like a cool washcloth on her forehead or other parts of her body. Keep them fresh as long as she wants them. Make sure to wring the cloth out thoroughly; dripping wet skin will annoy her.

READING THE SIGNS

Back off if your efforts annoy her. Her annoyance may pass quickly, or it may last hours. Either way, she still needs you by her side, ready to do what she wants.

Advocate and mediate for her with the hospital staff. Make sure you understand any professional suggestion before you okay it. If your partner wants medication to block the labor pains, tell the staff. But recognize (and help her understand) that many OB/GYNs will wait a half hour or so before giving the medications, to see if phase three is about to start.

Phase Three to Delivery

Phase three (of stage one) is the transition into stage two—the actual delivery. Remember that you're close to the goal line, so remind her how well she and the baby are passing all the yard markers.

As contractions get stronger and closer together, she may feel an irresistible urge to push. Help her to hold off until the OB/GYN says it's time. If the urge is overwhelming, and no one has examined her for a while, call a nurse and get the doctor in.

Be short and sweet in your words. Her concentration may be as intense as her contractions, so keep your coaching simple and specific. She may be particularly sensitive to anyone touching her, so look for her cues.

She may be so caught up in the contractions that she can't keep track of them. So, tell her when they start and stop, as well as their frequency. Hang in there! Delivery is just around the corner.

Make Way for Baby

Things move at a brisk pace after stage one of labor. But you probably won't notice. Many dads say that time slows down or becomes elastic once the OB/GYN says, "Push!"

I remember the surroundings of our delivery room in great detail, and remember many specific moments and movements—much more than normal for such a short span of time. The most vivid memory is seeing each of our children come out, actual people right from the start.

Even though events happen rapidly, you need to know what to do and when as you move through this brief and amazing moment in your life.

Elastic Momma, Queasy Poppa

If everything progresses the way it's supposed to, your partner's contractions have completely dilated her cervix and widened the mouth of her uterus for the baby to slip through. The contractions also push the baby's head down to the cervix, and right on through into the miraculously expandable vagina, which now takes on the function of birth canal.

Why "canal" and not "tunnel?" Perhaps because there are liquids and semi-liquids involved? Nevermind; now is not the time for grammatical or philosophical questions.

You're entering stage two of labor: delivery of the baby. Because delivery is messy—with probability of blood, poop, and goo—some men fear that they will falter or faint, failing their partners at the goal line. As my grandmother used to say (exaggerating her Bronx accent), "Yew shudn'd worry." In the heat of the moment, most fathers aren't fazed by the blood and commotion of a delivery room. The more focused you've been on helping your partner through labor, the more your gaze and attention zero in on your new baby; everything else falls away.

 DAD WORDS

No matter how many times I saw an ultrasound or felt the baby kick, it just wasn't real for me. Once I held my precious daughter in my arms and saw her with my own eyes, tears ran down my face while I said, "Look look, she's real! She's here." My wife just smiled and said, "I know. I've known for a long time."

—Dennis

How Much Pain Is Too Much Pain?

Labor hurts. That's the shortest, truest sentence about pregnancy. It has hurt as long as women have given birth. Cultures older than ours use herbs, prayers, rhythmic breathing, meditation, and other methods to diminish the pain and/or distract a mother from it.

In twenty-first century North America, the most common ways to reduce pain during an unproblematic labor are the two I list here:

- The breathing and relaxation techniques you learn in birthing classes
- Pain blocking drug

After continuing commands (from your OB/GYN and others) to avoid drugs while she's expecting, it may seem odd to use drugs on pregnancy's last day. Pain medication during labor triggers widespread, heated, often polarizing argument in the childbirth field. If your life is short on contentious debate, you can easily find hundreds of websites, pamphlets, and books on this question.

My opinionated Irish genes could deliver the definitive take on this dispute, but it's unlikely anyone would listen. Instead, let's briefly discuss the most common anesthetic techniques used in labor:

Epidural block. This type of anesthesia provides a pain-numbing drug that allows mom to stay awake and alert during labor and delivery. Mom sits up while a qualified professional puts a fairly long needle in her lower back. The needle allows a catheter to carry anesthesia into the epidural area just outside the mother's spine canal (hence the name). The procedure is usually short and uncomfortable; you need to hold your partner close and perfectly still. It's administered an hour or more before delivery, and can be used for some C-sections.

Spinal block. Doctors administer spinal blocks right before delivery. A pain numbing drug gets injected into the lower spinal cord. Spinals have longer-lasting side effects than epidurals.

Pudendal block. The doctor injects a pain killer into the vagina or perineum, usually before a forceps- or suction-aided delivery.

Demerol. This is a trade name and unofficial shorthand for several different systemic drugs called narcotic analgesics (medications similar to morphine). They're administered through an IV or a needle to reduce pain during active labor and have strong side effects.

General anesthesia. General anesthesia "puts you under" during major surgery. In childbirth, doctors use it for emergency caesarean deliveries and, very rarely, for vaginal births—although it was the standard method for years. Your grandmothers were probably out cold when your parents were born.

Dumping the Drug Debate

Proponents of "natural" childbirth urge women to forego pain medication during labor. They argue that women gave birth without drugs for eons. That's true, but as fathering guru Armin Brott says, "Moms also died from childbirth in much larger numbers; and doctors used to do surgery without anesthesia or antibiotics. There's no one 'right' way to go through childbirth."

If you and your partner decide to skip medication, that's great. During labor, she makes the call. (Don't argue with her; it's her body.) If she changes her mind, and opts for an epidural, that's great, too.

Don't believe anyone who says that you "failed" by using medications during labor. Childbirth is "right" when mom and baby make it through. Guilt and shame are irrelevant, useless, and just bad news.

As with every other major childbirth decision, discuss the pros and cons of pain-blocking with each other and your OB/GYN well ahead of time. But be flexible and respond to situations that arise when labor actually comes. If she's sure she wants drugs to numb the pain, don't debate—get the doctor.

Slow Poke Moms

Normally, a woman's body generates huge amounts of oxytocin when the cervix and uterus distend during labor. Oxytocin facilitates getting baby down the birth canal and out the chute.

If your partner seems stuck in the neutral, the OB/GYN may recommend jump-starting labor with synthetic oxytocin. He'll also induce labor if her water has broken and contractions haven't started, haven't gotten into a regular pattern, or there are other reasons to move things along. Your partner will get an IV solution with drugs usually known by brand names like Pitocin and Syntocinon.

Induced labor may create more pain for mom, increasing the need for pain blockers. Synthetic oxytocin can also increase the chances for fetal distress and a C-section. This is another issue for OB/GYN discussion ahead of time.

HEADS UP

Your OB/GYN might give your partner and/or your baby antibiotics to counteract bacteria in the vagina. Babies passing through an infected birth canal can catch the infection, so a course of antibiotics is not unusual. If mom has the active herpes virus, caesarean is the only choice to protect baby.

Stage Two and What to Do

In stage two, you do more of what you've been doing: encouraging, comforting, advocating for her with the staff, and soaking up the whole experience.

She may seem exhausted after all this labor and you may tire of keeping her energy up. But many expectant moms and dads get a sudden power burst from the deep recesses of their beings for this last big push. Once again, nature finds a way!

Push 'em Out, Shove 'em Out!

Once the OB/GYN says it's time to push, work closely with your partner to get her through each effort, just as you've been doing with contractions. Your OB/GYN may ask you to prop her up or otherwise support her body to facilitate delivery. If you're using a birthing tub, you'll be in the water with her.

Stay totally in tune with her and her current needs, while also following the lead and instructions of the professionals. This can be your toughest walk on the tightrope between advocacy and obstructionism, but if things are progressing smoothly, most dads find people in the delivery room are on the same page.

Stay loose physically and mentally. Don't lock your knees or stay in one position too long. Move around or stretch to release physical tension. That'll lessen her tension, save energy, and keep you more aware.

Some women say they don't remember hearing any doctor instructions, but they do remember their partners telling them what to do. Prepare to be the conduit from professional to mom at this stage, since she knows you better.

Your Delivery Party

Don't get distracted by who else is in the delivery room. You may have 18 neonatal nursing students, OB residents, and med students in to watch. We did, because our twins were the first vaginal delivery of multiples in more than a year at an inner city teaching hospital.

Far more normal is you, your partner, the doctor, and a nurse or two. However, you may want to have other special people in for the ride.

Leon's first child was his wife's second. Some people thought they were crazy to have his 14-year-old stepdaughter in the delivery room. However, big sister now has a deep bond with her brother after seeing him born firsthand. Afterward, she told her stepfather: "I hope I have small babies." Leon thought that bit of teen birth control was a major bonus!

Some new parents want a sibling, parent(s), or close friend to be part of the delivery experience. It is essential that the two of you discuss these arrangements with each other—and any/all of your invited guests—weeks before labor starts.

You have too much on your mind in the moment to juggle a guest list. If a relative or friend in the waiting room asks (or demands) to be let into the delivery room at the last minute, firmly decline. Tell them you and your partner have already arranged your birthing scenario and are not changing it now. If the person in question gets upset or hangs on to a grudge about this—it's their problem, not yours.

If you do have relatives or friends in the delivery room, make your expectations clear to them ahead of time. For example, make sure they understand that you will be the primary support and advocate for your partner. Other folks (including the health care pros) are there to lend a hand, not take your place.

The Crowning Moment

In a perfect world, the baby's head is down and comes out before anything else. As the heaviest part of the infant's body, nature aligns the head so gravity can lend birth a hand. It's a very tight squeeze to get that head through the cervical opening and birth canal, so the baby usually turns her head to fit.

Nature also makes her skull flexible and squishy, so it can fit through. That's why some babies seem to have slightly "pointy" skulls when they're born. (Please don't call her "Conehead." It doesn't last.)

There can be lots of time between crowning (when the top of her head appears) and actual birth, so it may feel like you're stalled. Be patient. Eventually, things progress.

The person delivering the baby will either coax the rest of the head out, or just wait for it to drop into his hands. After that, mom, baby, and delivery person conspire to wriggle the shoulders out. The remaining, narrower body parts easily slide down the path that the head so considerately plowed. Drum roll, please: you have yourselves a baby.

Episiotomy

An episiotomy is a small incision in the mother's perineum, the tissue between the anus and vulva. The doctor numbs the area before making the cut that makes the vaginal opening wider. This leaves more room for the baby's head to pass through. After the baby and placenta are delivered, mom has to stay put while the doctor sews up the incision.

However, the American College of Obstetricians and Gynecologists now discourages routine episiotomies, because longitudinal research shows that babies do just as well without it, and that mothers may do even better. Women seem to have fewer vaginal and urinary infections without an episiotomy, as well as less blood loss and lingering pain. They also have less intercourse-related pain after pregnancy, and don't wait as long before having sex after childbirth—which may matter to you both!

Talk it over with your OB/GYN, and ignore anyone who suggests you copped out by having one.

Where's Daddy?

You may have several options during the moment of birth itself. Be sure to talk about them with your partner and OB/GYN ahead of time, completing the necessary arrangements and pregame preparation.

Some facilities allow the father to actually deliver the baby if there are no complications. This gives you the thrill of having your baby drop right into your hands as she leaves your partner's body. The OB/GYN is right next to you all the time, in case you or the baby have any difficulties. The one drawback is that you must (obviously) leave your partner's side to do this.

If you don't deliver yourself, you may choose to stand over the doctor's shoulder for a close-up look at the birth. This position also means leaving your partner's side. If you capture still or video pictures from this angle, don't let this interfere with experiencing this fleeting moment. It's literally a once in a lifetime event; even if you have other children, you will never see this child born again. Flikr images will never top the images in your memory.

DAD WORDS

I had a camera in one hand and my wife's hand in the other. Breath, breath. Don't push yet. Push. Seeing the baby's head appear in the birth canal was almost a supernatural thing. It was like I was at the scene watching God blowing the breath of life into Adam's nostrils. Watching creation. It was indescribable really.

—Andy

Many hospitals position a mirror so the mother can watch the baby emerge, something she can't see on her own. A mirror also allows you to see the birth while staying by her side.

A few OB/GYNs and/or hospitals require the father to stay at the mother's head. Most places give you some leeway to move around the delivery room. But always remember that your first obligation is to your partner and helping her push the baby out.

Witnessing the delivery of your child can make your head spin. Remember to breathe! Periodic relaxation (deep breaths, a loud "aahhhh") helps you stay open to all that's happening, and makes you optimally useful to your partner and the baby. If you feel faint, sit down, and tell the nurse or OB/GYN how you feel. They may have a sugar source nearby to restore your equilibrium.

After the baby emerges, get your hands on her as soon as you can. If possible, have the doctor allow you to hand the infant to mom, and then lean in for a magical moment of connection and closeness.

Umbilical Options

The baby arrives with his umbilical cord attached to the placenta, which is still inside mom. Doctors and midwives usually check things like lung ventilation and wait varying lengths of time (another source of childbirth debate) before cutting the cord.

Many fathers want to cut the cord themselves. If the birth is smooth, few doctors object. In fact, many doctors even encourage dad to cut the cord during a caesarean.

Make arrangements with the OB/GYN beforehand (definitely list "dad cuts cord" on your birth plan), and make sure this step isn't forgotten in the rush of delivery. The OB/GYN will put two clamps on the cord, and you cut between them. It takes some effort, but the experts are standing by, so don't be afraid.

If there are no complications, cutting the cord can be a powerful rite of passage for you. It is an intimate, symbolic, and amazing way to cross the threshold into fatherhood. Part of our fathering heritage is introducing our child to the larger world, helping her learn that she can survive, thrive, and be at home there. Cutting the umbilical cord can physically represent the start of that process and your lifelong commitment to your child.

But, if the thought of taking scissors to your baby makes you squeamish, don't worry. It's fine to let the doctor do it, and you'll still have many ways to bond with the child.

You and your partner must also decide ahead of time whether to keep the blood remaining inside the umbilical cord and placenta. Cord blood is rich in stem cells, so medical science is developing ways to use it (and cord tissue) to help treat some genetic illnesses later in the child's life.

Storage isn't cheap. It can cost up to $3,000 to process the blood and tissue—and then another $250 a year or more to store it in a specialized laboratory's cryogenic tanks.

The doctor collects the blood (and/or tissue) from the cord within a few minutes of cutting it. The hospital then ships the material off to the storage lab you chose.

Discuss this option thoroughly with your OB/GYN beforehand. If you wait until you're in the delivery room to decide, it's probably too late.

Apgar and Co.

Your child gets an Apgar test one minute after birth, and again five minutes after birth. Virginia Apgar, MD, the first woman professor at Columbia University's medical school, invented this simple, effective diagnostic tool in the early 1950s.

With a good knack for PR, Dr. Apgar assigned each letter of her name to an important aspect of newborn health. On a scale of 0 (signs of trouble) to 2 (everything is rosy), a nurse or doctor will rate the following characteristics of your baby:

- **Appearance:** The color of the newborn's skin. Pink gets a 2 and blue a zero.
- **Pulse:** Baby gets a 2 for a pulse of more than 100 beats per minute.
- **Grimace:** The baby's reflexes are evaluated by his crying, response to stimulation, and irritability. He actually gets higher scores if he's irritable, which may be why they call it "grimace."
- **Activity:** Rating of how much the baby moves his arms and legs, an indication of muscle tone.
- **Respiration:** How regular his breathing is and if he cries without much effort.

As you can see, the Apgar is a timesaving, non-invasive tool for health care pros to determine if the baby is getting enough oxygen or is under other undue stress. If a nurse is butting in to look closely at the baby, she's probably doing the Apgar, so be ready for it.

We're Not Done Yet! Stage Three

Remember stage three of labor? (See Chapter 6 if you don't.) It gets less attention than the other two stages, but delivering the placenta is necessary nonetheless. In another of nature's wonders, the placenta separates itself from the uterus wall when the child is born. Its work complete, it vacates the premises after the cord is cut.

Fortunately, your partner's uterus still has contractions after birth, and those force the placenta down to the cervix. However, she may still have to do more pushing to force the placenta out. In most cases, this is a simple matter, and it seems to happen almost incidentally; you two are absorbed in the new baby.

But it may require some conscious work and distract her (and you) from being with the baby. Help her focus, get it over with, and then get back to your little one.

If you want to see the placenta, ask. It's pretty amazing to see the only organ that the body produces and then discards.

DAD WORDS

Love isn't a state of perfect caring. It is an active noun like struggle. To love someone is to strive to accept that person exactly the way he or she is, right here and now.

—Fred Rogers

A Change in Plans

Childbirth doesn't always go smoothly or according to expectations. Millions of factors must line up just right over the many months of pregnancy, and there are some things that simply cannot be controlled or accounted for.

Fortunately, we live in a time and culture with frequent and incredible advances in obstetrics and neonatology. This section addresses (very briefly) the most common things that happen when childbirth doesn't follow nature's preferred pattern of labor and delivery.

Caesarean Sections

A caesarean section is surgery. As surgeries go, it's fairly straightforward; the doctor opens up the mother's abdomen, then cuts into the uterus and lifts the baby out. The surgeon knows just what to look for in there!

General anesthesia is still common for this surgery, but a woman can often have a spinal block instead, so she is awake when the baby is born. (It's still called "birth" even though the baby doesn't enter the world through the vagina.)

It usually takes longer for a woman to recover from a caesarean than from vaginal childbirth. An abdominal incision takes more time to heal than an episiotomy, and she'll face weeks of restrictions on lifting—which means you'll need to carry that load.

It is much more common now for dad to be in the operating room for a caesarean birth, so he can provide support and see and hold the newborn.

If you get good, consistent prenatal care, your OB/GYN will know better whether your partner is at risk for having trouble delivering vaginally. He may recommend a scheduled caesarean in order to head off danger to mom and child.

A caesarean may also come into play if the fetus is in some sort of distress, and the mother hasn't reached full term or is not yet in active labor. It's not uncommon for premature babies to be delivered by caesarean.

If a woman's labor is stuck in stage one for many hours, and the OB/GYN is concerned about her health and/or the baby's, he may opt for an emergency caesarean. Same thing if the baby is in a dangerous position inside the uterus, such as feet first.

No one likes to go the caesarean route, but it may be the only way to the ultimate goal. Dr. Joy Dorscher says, "If anything goes wrong, it may seem as if we overreact in taking precautions. But, as a delivering physician, you hire me to watch for problems and take precautions, so that's what I do."

Caesarean procedure has improved over the years, which is good news for you and your partner. Most of the time, the incision is so low on the abdomen that no scar will show when she is clothed (even in a bikini). The incisions are smaller, too, and done in a way that increases the odds that she can deliver vaginally next time she's pregnant—probably the most important improvement. Still, many doctors won't go that route, and if your partner has had two C-sections, she'll need one for any future birth.

Dad's Caesarean Role

A caesarean section, especially an emergency one, is scary for dad and mom. You know this isn't the way it's supposed to go, and realize that your partner and/or baby are in some degree of trouble. Plus, you know that major surgery is risky in and of itself.

However, the vast majority of caesarean sections are successful and, by the standards of surgery, uneventful. The professionals around you have done this many times before. Ask questions, but keep your eye on the goal, which is doing what's necessary in time.

Some hospitals won't let a father into the surgery at all. Others require you to take a caesarean preparation class, which you obviously can't do on the day of the surgery. So be sure to discuss the caesarean scenario with your OB/GYN and hospital ahead of time. If they aren't willing to let you into a caesarean, find another birthing team.

Here's what to expect during a caesarean:

- You probably won't see your partner prepped for surgery.
- You will probably get much less attention from the professionals than during a vaginal delivery. Don't get in the way, but make your presence known. Ask questions, politely and judiciously.

- You will stand next to your partner's head, especially if she's awake for the surgery. Your job is to be the same supportive, encouraging, can't-wait-to-see-our baby guy you planned to be in the delivery room.

- If the baby doesn't have pressing medical needs, insist that you hold him and, if possible, give him to your partner for nursing.

- Cut the cord. You should discuss this with the OB/GYN beforehand, but there's no reason you can't cut the umbilical cord after a successful caesarean.

> **HEADS UP**
>
> The baby is coming out of your partner's body, so she gets to decide how much discomfort is too much. You're there to care for her, not decide for her. For example, if you think it's time for a C-section, talk to the OB/GYN first—and let the doctor bring it up with your partner. She needs your unconditional support, even when you'd rather spare her any more pain.

Breech Birth

Breech means the baby is not in position to exit head first, as nature, mom, and baby prefer. But life, and childbirth, doesn't always work that way.

In a frank breech, the baby's feet are doubled up by her head and her butt is at the cervix, or in medical terms, "in the presenting position." Traverse breech means the baby is lined up sideways in the uterus, with his back toward the birth canal. Incomplete or footling breach means that the baby is positioned to exit one foot first. If the presenting body part has dropped into the pelvis or against the cervix, that's a problem.

An OB/GYN can try to manipulate the baby into a better position by reaching up the birth canal and/or by maneuvering the mother's body. If that doesn't work, you can be pretty sure you're off to the operating room for a caesarean.

Two other presenting position problems are placenta previa, where the placenta covers the uterine opening and blocks the baby's exit, and a prolapsed umbilical cord, where the cord is tangled dangerously around the baby or crimped so that the baby's lifeline is threatened. Both conditions usually mean a caesarean.

Don't Try This at Home, If You Can Help It

In very rare circumstances, you may have to deliver your partner's baby alone. Do everything you can to avoid this scenario. But safety comes first in childbirth, so don't drive to the hospital in a hurricane or ski there in a blizzard. If your partner is through stage one and absolutely cannot keep herself from pushing, or if any part of the baby is crowning—you're the man.

 HEADS UP

Childbirth is not as tidy or speedy as it appears on TV. Private parts (childbirth's center of action) are usually taboo on TV, so emergency deliveries feature neatly placed blankets and spotless surroundings— even if mom and dad are in a horse barn (see *Bones,* season 7, episode 7). Adjust your expectations accordingly.

Stay calm and, if you can, call 911; those dispatchers are trained to talk you through a do-it-yourself delivery over the phone. That call also gets an ambulance and/or police officer underway, and prepares the hospital for your arrival (you'll have to go eventually). EMTs and cops are trained in delivering babies, so welcome them whenever they get there.

Make sure you and your partner are in the warmest, safest, cleanest place you can find. If indoors, turn the heat up all the way. Use blankets or anything else you can find to keep her (and eventually the baby) warm.

Position your partner comfortably on a soft surface, like a mattress. Let her push the baby's head out the birth canal and into your hands—resist the urge to pull him out. Gently support the head, and tell her to keep pushing as you guide the rest of the body out. Don't pull or twist the baby's body.

If the umbilical cord is wound around the neck, slowly pass it over the baby's head; don't pull or cut it. If necessary, do infant CPR or resuscitation—one more reason to take a CPR class! (Most "I-can't-wait" babies deliver without many complications.)

Immediately wrap the baby up in dry blankets and rub him dry. The rubbing stimulates blood flow and breathing. Plus, even in a warm room, a baby will chill quickly if still covered with fluids. Have your partner start breast-feeding right away. It helps the baby, and the skin-to-skin contact keeps him warm. (But keep a blanket over mom and baby.) Breast-feeding also contracts the uterus, reducing bleeding and stimulating the placenta to exit. Have her keep pushing, so that you can deliver the placenta, and then keep it for a physician to examine.

If you think an ambulance will get you to the hospital soon, leave the umbilical cord alone. If it will take longer than an hour or two to get medical attention, you'll have to cut the cord. Sterilize two pieces of string and a knife or scissors. Tie a piece tightly around the cord, four inches (or about the width of your hand) from the baby's belly. Then tie the second string tightly around the cord six inches away from the baby, and then cut it between the two knots with the sterilized knife or scissors. Don't do anything else with the cord. Then get all of you to a doctor as soon as possible.

And don't do any of this unless you have absolutely no other option.

Tweet or Consequences

In 1980, I spent close to an hour calling distant family members on a hospital pay phone before I finally reached anyone. (If you've never heard of a pay phone, check with Google or the ancient history museum for a picture.) Voicemail launched that same year, but no relatives had it, and I wasn't about to just leave a message. Until she died, my grandmother bragged widely that she was the first to know!

Now, you can Twitter and Facebook real-time updates for every stage of your baby's birth. But make sure you don't "Tumblr" into hard feelings when spreading the word on social media.

> **EXTRA POINT**
>
> Be sure to write down phone numbers for your closest family and friends and bring them with you. If the hospital limits cellphones, Siri can't place your calls. With all the distractions of a newborn, a list of your social media usernames and passwords can also help.

Develop a broadcasting plan with your partner before you go into labor. Are there special family members and friends that you want to tell in person or over the phone, before they StumbleUpon the news in cyberspace?

Do you want to post status updates about labor itself? If so, does your partner want veto power over messages like "Another contraction, so momma is being a real pain in the butt right now?"

If posting distracts your attention from focusing on your partner at any point, stop. A clever quip or whacky photo simply isn't worth it—or the grief you may get about it later.

Some parents post the news and images ASAP, and others wait until later, after they name the baby and talk to their closest loved ones. The choice is yours; just be sure to choose your social media strategy together. And use discretion; before hitting 'send," remember that those words and images will live forever on the web.

The Least You Need to Know

- Keep a thick skin; Mother and baby are more important than your pride.
- Participate as fully as you can in the birth by delivering the baby and cutting the cord, even with a caesarean.

- Prepare for what you want during delivery, and prepare to adapt to circumstances that arise.
- As a last resort, you can deliver your baby; nature provides.
- Spread your good news widely—and wisely.

Father's Day Is Here

In This Chapter

- Adjusting to your new family
- Mastering basic baby care
- Helping mom cope
- Establishing boundaries

Coming home with your first baby may feel a bit surreal. It may seem like you're just playing house, and it takes a few hours (or days) to fully realize that you really are going to stay parents from here on out. You may still be on the job 30 or 40 years later, although the day-to-day parenting demands will be far lighter!

Ask for help and guidance from family, friends, and health professionals during these early days. Remember, however, that your relationship with your baby is unique and some—including lessons learned from mistakes—you have to find out on your own.

Babies Don't Break

When you bring your newborn home, your parenting antennae are hyper-sensitive to anything he does or doesn't do. That's one way nature helps you meet the needs of this completely dependent little person.

When we brought Mavis home from the hospital, she fell asleep immediately. We checked on her cradle every 5 to 10 minutes to see if she was breathing. After three hours, we called the doctor, worried that she hadn't woken up yet. He said "Don't worry, coming home from the hospital can wear out a baby."

Mavis kept sleeping and we kept calling the doctor every two hours. Finally, he said, "Live by this motto for the next few years: Never wake a sleeping child if she's not sick." In the end, Mavis slept 11 hours—and never slept that long again.

Because your senses are heightened while you and the baby get used to each other, you may sometimes feel like you're overreacting, or going through wild mood swings. You are. Don't worry about it. You, your partner, and your baby all have a new life, and it takes some getting used to.

Call Me Unpredictable

As you adjust to this major life change, keep a balance between what you see and feel today and what's happening over the long term. Pretty soon, you'll get the hang of important skills, like not reading too much into the baby's routine—because that routine will turn upside down with little or no notice.

That's entirely normal. If your baby is in generally good health, his patterns may change from day to day or week to week, sometimes suddenly.

DAD WORDS

There's no harm in a child crying: the harm is done only if his cries aren't answered. If you ignore a baby's signal for help, you don't teach him independence. What you teach him is that no other human being will take care of his needs.

—Dr. Lee Salk

Just remember the long-term picture. Overall, this first year is a steady arc of growth in the baby's size, strength, and cognitive ability. Your baby will experience more growth and development in year one than in any other period of his life.

Have you ever tried to learn language or had to do months of physical therapy to regain post-injury range of motion? Not easy for most adults.

Yet, over the next year, this little lump of baby will begin to master one of the world's most complex languages—and learn to crawl and/or walk for the first time. Pretty damn impressive. Keep that amazing feat in mind as you go through the sometimes-confusing starts and stops of everyday baby care.

Don't let hordes of parenting and baby information stampede you into a panic. Resources for parents of newborns are valuable when used in moderation. In their thoroughness, books, magazines, and websites tend to cover every possible disease and hazard, even the improbable ones. This approach can prompt some parents to worry that every one of those problems is happening to their baby. Read to be informed, and take things with a grain of salt. Rely on nearby professionals (especially the pediatrician) more than the impersonal web for your own situation(s).

Holding the Baby

Feel a bit terrified about picking up and holding your tiny infant? Normal. As we discussed back in Chapter 1, most guys don't get much practice with this skill as boys or young adults.

Nature adapts to new father nerves by making babies flexible and resilient. If you handle the baby with confidence and care, he will be safe—and so will you.

Let's assume the baby is lying on his back on the changing table or crib, and that you're right-handed. Picking the baby up is a three-step process:

1. Put your right hand under his neck, supporting his head so that it doesn't flop around.

2. Put your left hand under his butt; don't be afraid to roll him a little to get your hands in place.

3. Lift with both hands, keeping his head at least a little bit higher than the feet.

Okay, you're holding the baby out at arm's length—now what do you do? Try moving gently into one of these three holds:

Squirmy football. Place his head in the crook of your elbow, hold him close to your body (somewhat like a pigskin), and support his butt and upper legs with your hand.

Cuddle. Bring the baby toward you, with his face facing you. With one arm supporting the head and the other on the butt, hold him close to your chest. Turn his head slightly (so he can breathe) and tuck it into the indentation between your shoulder and pecs. Breathe deeply and give a gentle hum, purr, or growl as you exhale; those vibrations in your chest can comfort the baby.

Bragger. Bring the baby toward you, but with his face facing outward. Put a hand under his butt and let the knees dangle, using your hand as his seat. Place his head gently against your chest. Move your "head" hand out and place it over his belly or chest. Keep a firm but gentle grip and support his head with your chest. The Bragger lets the baby look out at the world—and allows you to show him off.

HEADS UP

Baby Gabe and his unnamed, right-handed dad give an excellent 45-second "how to hold a newborn infant" demonstration at http://youtu.be/sVS-VvLMxvo.

I was nervous during the first few transfers from pick up to a "hold" position, but you'll master this quickly if you stay clam and confident.

Hint: There's nothing quite like feeling your baby relax totally and melt into your arms or chest.

When laying the baby back down, retrace your steps. Start by putting one hand under his head and neck, with the other under his butt, and lower with both hands. Well done!

The Kid's First First Aid Kit

Now that your baby is at home with you, you should have a well-stocked first aid kit in your home. You can buy ready-made kits, or assemble your own.

Start with information; include the phone numbers for your pediatrician, hospital, local poison control center, and relatives or friends you can ask for help in an emergency. Here's what else you should stock in your kit:

- An infant thermometer
- Baby pain and fever reducer (such as acetaminophen or ibuprofen) recommended by your pediatrician
- Nasal aspirator bulb
- Small tweezers (for splinters and such) and scissors
- Rubbing alcohol swabs to clean thermometers, tweezers, and scissors
- Antibiotic ointment for cuts and scrapes
- Irrigating eye wash
- Saline nose drops to clear stuffy noses
- Aloe gel for burns
- Adhesive bandage strips in assorted sizes
- Gauze rolls and pads, along with first aid tape
- Sterile cotton balls
- Oral syringe or other tool to give medicine
- Electrolyte fluids (like Pedialyte) to rehydrate a baby with diarrhea
- A first-aid manual

Check with your doctor to see what else to include in your first aid kit; she may have guidance and suggestions designed for your specific location and situation.

Of course, the first rule in a major emergency is to call 9-1-1. They can get help headed your way and talk you through emergency procedures over the phone.

If Daddy Could Breastfeed ...

A baby who gains weight and wets his diaper every few hours is probably getting enough to eat. Breastfed babies tend to eat more often than bottle-fed ones, but the difference isn't always huge. Why does your infant eat so frequently?

- He doesn't have a big stomach.
- His rapid growth consumes calories like a campfire consumes ice cubes.
- He needs to gain body fat to keep him warm.
- He's just learning to suck, so his mouth may grow tired before his tummy is full.
- He can't handle solid food for a few more months.

If your baby is born in the hospital, use those few hours or days to learn from the most experienced infant care professionals. Take advantage of the neonatal nurses and other hospital staff; they can give tips for holding the baby, getting him to sleep, encouraging him to suck, and other important new parent skills. Our twins spent three weeks in the neonatal ICU. While stressful, that experience also allowed the staff many chances to coach us on infant tricks!

Roll with the flow on the days he has to eat 10 times in 24 hours; getting annoyed won't change how hungry he is. Frequent feeding means frequent interruption of your sleep. Some dads think that this is mom's problem (especially if she's breastfeeding), because it's mom's job to keep junior full.

Dad-Baby Bottlenecks

Those dads who think feeding falls to mom alone are wrong, even though you can't share breastfeeding equally—no matter how hard you try! Duh. But, you and your partner can arrange breastfeeding to include you, rather than reinforce a pattern that leaves you on the outside looking in.

Here are some ways to do it:

- Mom breastfeeds and dad burps the baby.
- Once the baby can handle it without disrupting breast-feeding, use a breast pump to express mom's milk for a bottle.
- Dad uses that bottle to feed the baby. This builds dad-baby intimacy, and gives mom a break.

By this time in your parenting, you and your partner probably have heard every side of the so-called "breast vs. bottle" debate. New parents have three choices:

- Feed the baby only at mom's breast.
- Use infant formula manufactured to provide the nutrients most babies need.
- Use both formula and breast milk. (Don't give your baby milk from other animals, like cows, until much later.)

Her Breasts Work Fine for Me!

There's widespread agreement that breast milk is better overall for your baby than formula. Breastfeeding adapts to the baby's key needs; for example, in the first few days, it reinforces the baby's immune system. Breast milk helps reduce food allergies and supplies fatty acids that formula doesn't have. It is easier on the baby's digestion, so he has less smelly poops. It comes from a person who shares the baby's DNA.

Breastfeeding is also convenient, once your partner has mastered the skill. Her breasts are always with her, so you don't have to fill a diaper bag with formula cans or sterilize tons of nipples and bottles—just remember to bring mom along. However, as you've figured out by now, breastfeeding requires that mom be present. That can become a burden for her and an inconvenience when you want or need to take the baby someplace alone.

In addition, mastering the skill of breastfeeding can be difficult for a variety of reasons. Your partner and the baby may have trouble getting in sync with each other. She may develop raw skin, infections, or blisters on her nipples. The feeding schedule may exhaust mom (especially if you have more than one baby).

Remember:

- Just because your breasts don't lactate for the baby doesn't mean you can't help breastfeed.
- Your partner has had breasts for years; but she's never used them to feed a baby before. Don't expect her to be an expert.
- You and your family will be fine even if breastfeeding doesn't work out.

Mom and baby may get going seamlessly from day one—or it could take weeks to get in synch. Your baby has to learn how to "latch" onto mom's breast and suck consistently to get sufficient nourishment. Mom has to learn how to relax baby and herself, while coaxing baby to suck. This is new territory for all three of you. They are her breasts, so follow her lead and provide your unconditional support.

READING THE SIGNS

Most communities have lactation coaches or consultants to teach new moms good breastfeeding strategies. Le Leche League International (lalecheleague.org) or your pediatrician can recommend someone to help and encourage your partner. Welcome these folks into your home.

Your job is to be very, very supportive, even when you feel overwhelmed by how hard it seems for your partner and the baby, and by how little direct action you can take to solve the problem.

Simple things can help your cause. For example, don't get hung up watching the clock. The length of a particular feeding and the interval between feedings matters less than your natural parenting instincts. If baby is rooting around or giving his "feed me" cry, feed him—even if you just did.

Most important, tell your partner that she is bonding with the baby and is being a successful mother, even if she struggles with breastfeeding.

Bottled Magic

Using bottles—of pumped breast milk or formula—is fabulous for fathers. Just wait until you get your infant to suck smoothly. When you hold him close as he settles for your feeding, your feeling of satisfaction, connection with baby, and pride in providing him life's essentials will soar.

It's actually fairly easy to feed your infant. Start with the Squirming Football hold I described previously. Then, sit down in a comfortable chair, propping your left elbow (if you're a righty) on a pillow or the arm of the chair. Hold baby close, and use your right hand to hold and insert the bottle. You can stimulate his suckling instinct by gentling rubbing the nipple across his lips or stroking his cheek with your middle finger.

I'm a huge proponent of expressing breast milk so dad can feed the baby. But fair warning: some people may give you grief for doing it. A few breastfeeding advocates argue that interrupting direct mommy-nipple-to-baby feeding lessens the milk's immunological value. The doctors I know don't agree. But even if it were so, I believe that the feeding bond between dad and baby generates enormous physical, emotional, and psychological benefits that help build a healthy child.

And let's get something straight about infant formula. As your pediatrician can also tell you, there are very good reasons (including the mother's and/or baby's health) that parents opt for formula. If you go the formula route, enthusiastically grab the chance to share more equally in feeding your child. And don't believe anyone who tells you or your partner that you are failing your baby with formula!

Burping and Spitting Up—Yum!

Since your infant is very new at this suckling business, he consumes air along with his food. This produces bubbles and air pockets in his tummy that causes distress, fills up space he needs for additional nourishment, and creates a mild form of acid reflux. Hence, feeding an infant always involves a bit of burping.

As we look out across the vast fellowship of fathers, we see men who take as much pride in the shock value of their burps and belches as they do in the volume and fragrance of … the jet streams they fire from their backsides. While your baby may rip a really loud one occasionally, he doesn't burp (or fart) to get attention until he is about 10.

You need to burp your infant once or twice during a feeding and right after the feeding is finished. Otherwise, you'll have an unhappy, in-pain person in your hands promptly.

There is no single burping method that works all the time for every baby. Some infants respond to gentle rubbing, others to gentle patting. Hard whacks on the back are not good, despite what you've seen in the movies.

EXTRA POINT

When burping, always have one or two cloth diapers close by to help reduce the mess. They won't eliminate it, however; be prepared to wash your clothes more often than normal over the next few months.

Try holding the baby close to you, with his head peeking just over your shoulder. Pat or rub his upper and/or lower back gently. You'll have to experiment at first to see what pattern produces a burp most quickly.

Another good method is to place the baby face down on your lap, making sure to support his head. Rub or pat his upper and/or lower back gently from this position. Once he gets his burp(s) out, pick him back up for more feeding, or to prepare him for whatever is next in his day.

Many of an infant's burps also produce the aromatic liquid that polite people call "spit up." Your baby's lower esophageal sphincter—the valve between his esophagus and stomach—isn't mature yet, so some tummy fluids scoot back up where they came from. This is normal for the first year or so, although it tends to taper off after about four months. Spit up is different from projectile vomiting (caused by sickness) because … well, spit up doesn't project.

When our twins were babies, our 10-pound mutt often licked their bibs after burping, reducing the wiping up we needed to do. My wife and most doctors don't recommend this method; I plead the Fifth.

Changing a Diaper

Considering how much scatological humor boys use, why do so many of us freak out at changing diapers? Think of this as the opportunity to become an expert; after a few tries, you'll know more scatology (the study of fecal excrement) than the average bear.

For his first few days, the baby's fecal excrement will look somewhat Martian; heavy on the green coloring, with an otherworldly texture and odor. That's normal. Before long, his poop will look and smell more familiar, but will remain looser than an adult's.

Chances are good that someone else (like a nurse) will install your baby's first diaper. The unavoidable result is that the first time you change a diaper, it will already contain something. Ready? Clothespin on nose? Here goes:

Step 1: Prepare your tools. Make sure your work area is safe, clean, and unobstructed. Put the clean diaper, washcloth, baby wipes, and other tools within easy reach. Have a safe spot to set the dirty diaper aside.

Step 2: Lay the baby down on his back on a waterproof surface in a safe place (like the changing table or the floor). Undo the diaper's tabs or snaps, and pull the front half of the diaper downward, freeing the baby's legs. Holding his ankles gently, pick up his legs so you can pull the rest of the diaper from under his butt. If the diaper is wet, but not poopy, breathe a sigh of relief. If it's poopy, breathe wisely. Set the dirty diaper aside; you'll deal with it later.

Step 3: Notice all the cracks and crevices on and between the baby's legs. Poop and pee residue fills all of them, thanks to the diaper mashing everything the baby produces. Crevices vary from girls to boys, but you must clean out each one thoroughly with a soft washcloth or baby wipes. Leave anything behind, and baby's skin will become irritated within the hour. Do not shortcut; you will pay for it later with major-league diaper rash. No, you won't get diaper rash, but your baby's screams will make you feel like you did. Once you've wiped everything out, gently wipe his skin completely dry before moving on. If baby has diaper rash, apply ointment now (I talk more about diaper rash in the next section).

Step 4: Once again, hold baby's ankles to lift his butt up. With your other hand, slide the new, clean diaper underneath. Put the baby down so that his back waist and the diaper's top lines up with each other. Pull the bottom part of the diaper up through his legs, and onto his belly, fitting it snuggly into place. He will squirm and wrestle during this operation. Remain calm and gentle.

HEADS UP

Remember the ancient diaper-atic theorem: snugness and leakiness are in direct inverse relationship.

Next, snap or Velcro the diaper into place. Dress the baby again and either hand him to another adult or set him in a safe place while you deal with the dirty diaper and your now-dirtied tools.

Step 5: Toss all used baby wipes and disposable diapers in a plastic bag, and then tie or otherwise seal the bag. Every nose in your house and neighborhood will thank you. If you use a flushable liner, flush it (and the poop) down the toilet. If you use cloth diapers, hold one end of the diaper firmly while swishing the rest of it in the toilet to rinse off most of the poop. Do not let go while flushing; I used to work for Roto-Rooter—you do not want to go there.

Within a week, you'll be completing these 5 steps in 2 or 3 minutes. Your nose and stomach will adjust. And you'll develop many fun noises and faces to distract the baby during diaper time.

Diaper Rash

This bright and painful curse is usually caused by wet diapers, of which your baby will have plenty. Moisture against the skin forms bacteria that produce ammonia that irritates the skin. Diaper rash can spread if it isn't treated properly.

You may see diaper rash break out when the baby is taking antibiotics, begins solid foods, or has other changes in diet. If sores, blisters, pimples, or scabs develop in addition to the standard red, irritated skin, contact your doctor.

You treat diaper rash by changing diapers frequently, keeping baby's bottom and crotch completely clean (use mild soap and warm water), letting the diaper area air dry (don't use "baby" powder, it's easily inhaled and can cause breathing problems), and covering sore skin with diaper ointment.

You also prevent diaper rash by keeping the area clean and dry. Disposable diapers tend to generate more diaper rash than cloth ones; the plastic in disposables can make baby sweat more, adding to the crotch moisture. Cloth diapers can make things worse if they aren't soft and free of fragrances; wash cloth diapers only in very gentle, dye-free and fragrance-free detergent.

Just one more scatological question: what exactly does a bear do in the woods?

Caring for Mom

Your partner and her body have been through an unusual ordeal for most of the past year. Thanks to nature's post-natal hormone formula and the demands of new parenting, she's probably still stressing out. Listen and take her concerns seriously.

If she's has an episiotomy or C-section, her body needs time to heal. After a caesarean, most women have restrictions on what they can lift, and may even need bed rest. In these situations, you need to step up big time to carry the baby-care load, while also caring for her health. Ask for help from relatives and friends.

During the first few weeks, it's completely natural for her and you to feel out of sorts, blue, or even resentful of the demands of time and attention your baby is making upon you.

The Blue and the Grey

Postpartum depression isn't unusual for either parent, although it's more recognized (and may be more common) in women. This kind of moderate to severe depression may flare up during the first week after delivery or up to a year later. It is most common within the first 3 months after childbirth.

Even if neither parent develops depression, your mood will swing during baby's first days and months. Mom's hormone levels are still changing. Her body underwent major changes from pregnancy and delivery. Both of you have less sleep and free time than before. Your social and work relationships shift, and you naturally worry about your abilities as parents.

Therefore, expect some frustration, anxiety, tears, and irritation. These "baby blues" may lessen soon without the need for anything more than conversations with a trusted friend or relative.

Postpartum depression is more serious and lasts longer than the baby blues. Like any form of depression, the postpartum variety is serious, real, and needs treatment.

Some guys remain skeptical about the need for mental health treatment and think that depression is "all in your mind." I encourage those guys to read up on the last 10 years of brain research. It shows that traditional distinctions between physical and mental illness don't hold up. Problems like depression are now known to be biological and chemical disorders within the organ of the brain—they aren't imaginary or any less real than a broken leg. So if depression becomes a problem, don't try to fix it alone. If you or your partner feel unusually sad or unhappy, talk to your doctor.

Baby on Parade

Your new baby is a first for you. He's also a first for your family and friends—and may be a big attraction for others, including strangers.

Because you and your partner are dealing with a lot in the hospital and during your first days home, you have the authority to set limits with visitors and passersby.

If having loved ones over to help will ease your stress, invite them in! If visitors increase your stress, invite them to wait or to lend you a hand in some other way.

Let's say your nosey neighbor keeps knocking on the door, insisting on visiting mom and baby, but mom is too tired or blue for company. Explain to Ms. Nosey that baby can't come to play right now, and thank her for her interest and concern. Then ask if she can help you out by cooking a meal you can freeze, mowing your lawn, or running to the store for you in a pinch.

Talk directly and honestly with your relatives and friends, even if you're not used to doing so. That prevents you from having to switch on the burglar alarm during the day while you hide behind drawn window shades.

Make your limits and needs clear, while reminding loved ones that your limits and needs will change as the baby grows and you get your parenting legs. Some limits—like, don't visit the baby if you're sick—apply across the board. Others—like your need for privacy—may be more specific to your situation, personalities, and needs.

You will quickly learn the times of day that you, mom, and baby have the most energy and interest in socializing. Invite folks to visit during those times, and enjoy the fuss they make over the baby.

Me Time, Us Time

For the next 20 years or more, the way you and your partner spend your time will look different than before. Your child (or children) will need you to feed, clothe, and house them. Drive them to school, practice, prom, and college. Help them deal with monsters under the bed, broken hearts, and their own pregnancies.

DAD WORDS

An hour with your grandchildren can make you feel young again. Anything longer than that, you start to age quickly.

—Gene Perret

This brings the new challenge of finding time for your relationship with your partner, time for yourself, and time for your friends and other interests.

Many people say that the best thing a father can do for his children is to love their mother. Nevertheless, adults can be fabulous parents even if they no longer love each other.

For now, let's assume you and your partner are interested in continuing your relationship. You already know that relationships require time and attention, two resources that children consume voraciously. That means proactively making time to be alone with your partner—and not just for nookie.

Get a relative or sitter to take the baby for an hour so you can just hang out. Instead of trying to accomplish a major project during baby's naptime, grab some sleep (and not just for nookie).

Good you-and-me times can be short; a quiet conversation and cuddle while the baby naps. They might be medium-length, like a date night out for dinner and a movie (with the help of a babysitter). When your child gets older, you can sneak away for longer periods. Be realistic, though; as the late comic Erma Bombeck said: "For years, my husband and I advocated separate vacations. But the kids keep finding us."

The key is making the time. Since time doesn't make itself, this takes action.

You'll also need to show intention and attention to make time for your friends. But first—if you're serious about being a dad—accept the fact that your wild oats days of constant Clubbin' & Cruisin' are over. You can still hang and party with the guys, but not at the expense of your new family. And remember that mom also had a life before baby. Make sure your partner gets equal time to get away for time with her gal pals, too.

DAD WORDS

There's really no point in having children if you're not going to be home enough to father them.

—Anthony Edwards

Perhaps most important is making time for you, your health, and your well-being. Keeping your regular routine of exercise, reading, prayer, or other activities may now require sacrificing some sleep. The sacrifice is worth the effort if it feeds your balance, energy, and capacity to be present for your child and your family.

Dads get creative about integrating parenting and personal growth: running with the baby in his jogging stroller, praying while diapering or rocking the baby to sleep, and keeping the yoga mat unrolled for quick use during the baby's nap. Use your imagination while continuing to nurture yourself, your partner, and your relationships while nurturing your new child.

I'm So Frustrated, I Could Scream

When our daughters were infants, Nancy and I went to new parent classes offered by the local Early Childhood Family Education (ECFE) program. One day, the teacher asked, "Have any of you new parents ever felt like hitting your baby?"

I was incensed. "How could you even talk about that?" I demanded, "No one should ever hit a baby!"

"You didn't hear my question," the teacher replied. "I asked, 'Have you ever felt like hitting your baby?' not 'Have you ever hit your baby?' So tell me, haven't you ever gotten so frustrated by your babies' crying or not doing what you want that you felt like smacking them?"

Although I'd never struck my kids, I had to admit that I sometimes felt like it, especially during the worst colic episodes when it seemed like they'd never stop crying.

"That's my point," the teacher said. "It's normal and okay to feel like hitting them; it's never okay to actually hit a kid."

"If you don't admit that you sometimes feel like hitting them, then it's much more likely that you actually will hit them. If you do admit the feeling to yourself or someone else, then it's much easier to release your frustration in a healthy way that won't hurt your daughters or you. It can be something as simple as putting the baby in her crib, going out in the backyard, and yelling loudly to release the tension."

I tell this story not just to endorse ECFE classes (which I do heartily; go to them!), but to illustrate a very common experience new parents have.

Every parent does!

You will be exhausted from all the routine activities of baby-care. You will wish the house was clean and organized, which is usually impossible with a new infant. You will have moments when you feel so completely frustrated that you erupt in rage.

If we want to protect our babies, we have to recognize the difference between having a feeling and acting on that feeling. There is nothing wrong with feeling frustrated and angry about the challenges of childrearing. Right and wrong enter the scene when I decide what actions to take (and not take) when those feelings come.

We may not like to admit it, but feeling enraged does not make us hit someone or something. I choose to hit (or not hit) in response to my anger and stress. I have to understand the difference, knowing that it's okay to want to lash out, but not okay to actually lash out.

If you feel so resentful of your baby that you are tempted to hurt him, contact your physician immediately or call a parents' hotline or "warmline."

We want to protect our families. Nature, common sense, the wisdom of veteran parents, and our love for our children all combine to help us do that job well. We have a lot of resources to help honor and hold that special role of protector.

Go, Baby!

There's a wide range of "healthy" when it comes to a newborn's weight and length, which are affected by a wide range of factors, including term at birth, genetics, events during pregnancy, and more. It is also common for a newborn to lose some weight in the days following the stress of birth. He usually starts regaining the weight and then is off to the growth spurt races. Monitor the situation, and if you have concerns, ask the doctor.

His umbilical cord stump will fall off sometime during the first three weeks. There may be some drainage or bleeding (normal) and the spongy stump will change color as it dries up.

During your newborn's first month, he will stare at faces, and recognize some, including you and your partner. While his mind isn't yet developed enough to feel and demonstrate love, he will start attaching to you.

His vision will take in hordes of information from day one. That stimulates his brain development and prompts him to learn later physical skills like rolling over. It appears that babies prefer looking at faces more than the colors and patterns of crib mobiles and wallpaper—one more reminder that you are more valuable than any product, gimmick, or toy. He will even begin to follow your face with his eyes. So, give him plenty of face time. It's a great way to get to know each other and learn that he really does have a personality already!

DAD WORDS

A new father quickly learns that his child invariably comes to the bathroom at precisely the times when he's in there, as if he needed company. The only way for this father to be certain of bathroom privacy is to shave at the gas station.

—Bill Cosby

He will begin to lift his head during the first month, and may be able to hold it up. He will also cry. (*Hint:* This is a skill he keeps for a long time.) But even this early, you may be able to differentiate between his piercing "I'm hungry" scream and a "change my diaper" whimper. He may also coo, respond to your voice, and become more aware and alert.

Give the baby sponge baths during the first few weeks. She can't really hold herself well enough for a water bath (see Chapter 12 for details on bathing baby), and besides, you shouldn't submerge the umbilical cord stump in water.

Keep the umbilical stump dry, even if it means altering how and how often you diaper the baby. Clean the cord with mild soap and water, dry it thoroughly, and then use a Q-tip to wipe the base gently with alcohol. It will eventually fall away.

By the end of the first month, he will be sleeping a lot of the time, but not for long stretches. He may stay awake for an hour or more. Make sure you put him on his back when he sleeps.

The Least You Need to Know

- You can hold, feed, and change your baby with confidence and skill.
- Mom needs support and care during her first days as a parent; so do you.
- You can still have friendships, romance, and self-care.
- Your baby will start growing up right away.

Scoring: Sex (and Other Relations) for New Dads

In This Chapter

- Lighting your libido
- Enjoying sex during and after pregnancy
- Nurturing your changing relationships
- Securing your place in baby's life

Sex.

Sex. Sex. Sex. Sex. Sex. Sex. Sex. Sex. Sex.

Good, now that we have your attention, let's talk about how fatherhood affects your libido—and your most important relationships.

As much as women mock men for obsessing about sex, we really do understand how to assess our intimate relationships with something more than a cheat sheet marking "how often I have scored." We know that real intimacy involves psychological, spiritual, intellectual, emotional, and physical connection. We know that sexiness requires more than any single physical appearance.

After all, a meaningful relationship can't last long if it depends exclusively on either participant's cup size.

Although this chapter tackles some practical issues (like how to have intercourse while navigating a large baby bump), the discussion also encompasses the larger context of why you're having sex with your partner. You love her. So much so, that you're bringing a new human being into the world.

Lessons in Practical Physics: Sex During Pregnancy

Let's start by dispelling a lingering urban myth. Sex during pregnancy will *not* cause a miscarriage. Your partner's tough uterus muscles and all that amniotic fluid provide the baby with plenty of protection.

You can be sure of one other thing: if you're having sex with your partner while she's expecting, you can't get her pregnant. For many couples, freedom from worry about unintended pregnancy can lead to greater relaxation during foreplay and intercourse.

However, this doesn't guarantee smooth sailing in the weeks and months before her bump becomes an obstacle.

Early in her pregnancy, you two can be physically intimate the same way you were before. But, if she has morning sickness (a.k.a. nausea and vomiting), she may not be in the mood for romance very often.

DAD WORDS

Amnesia: The condition that enables a woman who has gone through labor to have sex again.

—Joyce Armor

As the pregnancy progresses and her belly grows, it's harder to reach familiar places in the old familiar ways. Intercourse will require several adjustments and even some giggles as you try to devise workable methods.

Throughout it all, her hormones will be on the march and her body working overtime to grow another person. Your hormones and attitudes are in flux, too, so it's smart to stay flexible.

Moaning Over Hormones

As you already know, pregnancy brings major physical and hormonal changes to your partner's body. You'll be very happy to learn about some of these. The others may be a bit more problematic.

Of course, morning sickness sucks—nausea and vomiting are certified turnoffs. Many women are very tired during the first weeks of pregnancy, which also dampens their appetite for sex. Some women struggle to reconcile their sense of sexuality and romance with their growing sense of being mothers. (Mothers don't have sex, do they? Our mothers certainly didn't!) This struggle may not be logical, but it is real.

On the other hand, when a woman has more energy, her "I can't get pregnant" feelings may fire up her libido. She may dream and fantasize about sex and want to have sex with you more often than before.

However, some women don't have increased sex drive during pregnancy. If your partner isn't hot to trot as often as you expected (or hoped), that doesn't mean there is something wrong with her. Recognize that her feelings may change as her hormones and body continue to change. Don't give up on her; she needs you to communicate with her more than ever now. And remember that you two are creating an incredible person … who will eventually pass through her vagina, deflating the bump, and leave the field open for you.

As with most other aspects of parenting, start with communication. Invite your partner to share her beliefs about sex and sexuality—especially her beliefs about sex during and after pregnancy. Pregnancy can bring a new level of closeness and intimacy that facilitates conversation about sexual fears, awkwardness, and discomfort. Openly discuss how each of you are responding to the physical and emotional changes. Listen to her and take her seriously.

As the pregnancy progresses, your partner's vagina and clitoris will become "engorged," increasing in lubrication and sensitivity. This is a big plus for your combined sexual pleasure. In addition, her orgasms may happen more readily and last longer than before. Intercourse may give her multiple orgasms during this period. Don't feel bad if you can't always keep up with her. If you're having sex from a desire for intimacy, joy, and love—you'll help her feel fabulous.

The "engorging" phenomenon also appears in most pregnant women's breasts. There are practical reasons for this—increased hormones and blood flow to prepare mom for feeding baby. Bonus!

During the first trimester, your partner's breasts are likely to become more sensitive. That can heighten her levels of pleasure, pain, and the line between them. Work together to maximize the pleasure (for both of you) and minimize the pain.

Enlarged and engorged breasts can give the both of you some nice new sensations. Many women feel especially sexy during pregnancy's middle months, as their juicier, plumper physiques broadcast their fertility and attractiveness.

You'll Poke the Baby's Eye Out (Not)

As her bump gets larger, it becomes more obvious (and real) to you that an actual baby really is inside there. It's normal for that knowledge to make you worry about hurting the baby during intercourse.

You won't hurt the baby, but there's a chance that intercourse may influence actual or potential problems in your partner's pregnancy. If that's your situation, you need to understand and follow her doctor's recommendations faithfully.

The doctor may tell you to hold off if your partner is at risk for miscarriage, or if you have an active sexually transmitted disease.

HEADS UP

Don't take any STD lightly. For example, if you have an outbreak of genital herpes, and your partner gets it for the first time while pregnant, there's a chance the baby can catch herpes while passing through the birth canal.

If your partner experiences any of the following, check with the doctor to see if they signal a problem for the pregnancy and/or your sex life (remembering which one is more important ... you know, right?):

- Unusual or persistent cramps
- Vaginal bleeding
- A weak cervix (the OB/GYN should be checking for this already)
- Placenta previa (her placenta is blocking the cervix)

READING THE SIGNS

Encourage your partner to talk about how intercourse feels during pregnancy. She may not want to disappoint you by acknowledging a problem. But if she's experiencing unusual vaginal discharge, bleeding, or pain—you and the doctor both need to know about it.

Tell her doctor or midwife about any concerns. Take comfort in the fact that they've heard it all before, so they won't be embarrassed or think you're a fool for asking. Of course, keep asking questions until you're sure you understand the reasons why the doctor advises against or restricts intercourse (or vaginal foreplay).

Ballooning

Dear *Idiot's Guide* Guy: So how do you have sex with a very pregnant woman?—Puzzled in Pocatello

Dear Puzzled: Creatively.

Physics creates some sexual challenges as your partner's belly gets bigger. The man-on-top "missionary" position simply doesn't work for intercourse anymore. But creativity—finding a way that works—can be a lot of fun.

Before we come to some penetrating solutions (what, you don't like double entendre?), let's look at some lovely coital alternatives.

There will be times when either you or your partner won't be in the mood to make love. Fortunately, there are many other ways to connect with each other physically and sexually. If intercourse is too painful or problematic, consider oral sex, masturbation, and creative foreplay for pleasure and intimacy. You can also find enormous connection, comfort, and satisfaction by snuggling together, hugging, kissing, saying how much you love her, massaging—and even talking about your feelings!

Many women feel less worried than usual about their bodies and their appearance during pregnancy. Sadly, women (and girls) face almost unrelenting pressure to obsess about the way their bodies look. Pregnancy may ease those anxieties, or even send them packing altogether. If so, the pregnant woman is likely to feel much better, more confident, and sexier. Yet another bonus for you!

Sex and the Bump

Once your partner's baby bump morphs into a mini-mountain, you have to adjust. Have fun experimenting while you find positions and activities that bring you together, bring you pleasure, and avoid pain.

One of the most common solutions is woman-on-top. If you've never done this before, it's simple. Lay on your back and support your partner as she lowers herself onto you. You'll have to both adjust your weight distribution, balance, and angles, but you can make it work. If your partner's breasts are easily aroused during her pregnancy, this is a great way to enjoy easier access to them during intercourse!

For a fun variation, try sitting on a chair—a very sturdy chair— while your partner lowers herself onto you. Again, you'll need to experiment, so be sure to enjoy the trial and error. If you need to stop momentarily to position a pillow, just remember that you now have an extra chance to "connect."

 HEADS UP

Pregnancy and anal penetration do not go together. Anal sex can spread bacteria to the vagina, which is bad for baby. Plus, it's very painful for a woman with hemorrhoids—fairly common during pregnancy.

The "spoon" is another variation that works well. Your partner lies down on her side, curling her body. You lie down behind her, copying her curl. Spooning is great for cuddling, whispering sweet nothings in her ear, and foreplay. It's also excellent for intercourse— you enter her vagina from behind. You won't be able to penetrate as deeply as you can with other positions, but that's just fine late in pregnancy, when deep thrusts are painful for her. There's just not much room left in there!

As she gets larger, your partner's hormones are working to loosen up her joints and ligaments. This is the body's way to make room for her rapidly expanding uterus. A major side effect is achiness, especially in her back. With looser joints and ligaments, her muscles have to work harder to hold everything together, which creates pain. Be conscious of these body changes as you explore sexual positions and activities.

Finally, here's one more good reason to embrace sex during pregnancy. A woman's orgasm releases hormones and other chemicals in her body. These are "happy" happenings that help her relax and feel great—which will, in turn, help the baby feel great. Plus, if your sexual relations are part of your continually growing relationship, that's great for baby, too.

Keep Your Eyes Offa Her!

There's something very sexy about a pregnant woman. In fact, there are numerous things! It may seem like her skin has changed and has a luminescent quality you've never seen before. Her growing breasts and belly may trigger intense pride in her fertility—and pride in your own virility.

The sexiness of a pregnant woman may also catch the attention of other men. Pregnancy is, after all, a very concrete sign that a woman is willing to have sex. Another guy might find a pregnant woman's voluptuousness titillating and exciting. So don't be surprised if other men flirt with your woman while she's pregnant. There appear to be some biological and evolutionary reasons for it.

Some scientists suggest that pregnancy prompts women to give off certain pheromones—hard-to-detect odorous substances. Your pet may pick upon this and change their behavior in response. Many pregnant couples notice a dog becoming more protective of mom, while a cat is more avoidant of her.

Mom-to-be's pheromones may also trigger changes in you as a man—a slight drop in testosterone and increase in prolactin. One theory holds that these hormonal changes make us feel and act more parental, with greater attraction to our mate and a greater desire to protect her.

Pheromones may play a small part in drawing attention from the guy standing next to her at the coffee shop. Do not fear (or get jealous). Her curves and pheromones have far more impact on you than anyone else—because you're exposed to them all the time. This is nature working to bond her together with you, not someone else.

So be proud—not jealous—of how hot she looks; it's working for you!

Sex After Childbirth: The Next Frontier

During the drama of the delivery room and the flood of logistics involved in establishing an infant at home, "doing it" may temporarily drop off your radar.

But as you get into a childcare rhythm, your thoughts may very well return to sex. As during the pregnancy, however, you and your partner may not always be in the same intimacy rhythm.

The impact of labor and delivery mean you can't rush things. Many OB/GYNs recommend waiting six weeks after childbirth to give mom's body time to fully recover from its little escapade. That can be frustrating. But just imagine pushing a child out through some orifice in your body—and how long it might take you to feel ready for vigorous activity.

If your partner had an episiotomy, torn perineum, or a C-section, she will need even more time to heal before you can have intercourse. Remember that the situation is temporary and no reason to do something stupid (or should we say really stupid) like playing the blame game or looking for sexual "satisfaction" elsewhere.

In fact, now is an ideal opportunity to explore the other aspects of intimacy: verbal, emotional, and spiritual. These not only make your relationship richer (and your parenting more fun), but they generally have a marvelous effect on the sex, once that mode of intimacy returns.

After childbirth, sex can bring up emotional and psychological challenges, and/or generate new depths of emotional and psychological connection. Start by realizing that a significant part of both of your identities changed dramatically—you are now parents!

One or both of you may sometimes feel like parenting and being sexual just don't go together. Also, your partner's body is now different, so you may both feel slightly different about it, especially as you cope with common (and temporary) phenomena like a sagging belly or milk flowing from her breasts during arousal.

Above all, communicate openly and lovingly with each other. That can be hard to do when you're both tired, on different schedules for sexual desire, and covered in spit up. Be patient, tender, and accommodating. If you and your partner become out of synch sexually, it's not because she's out to get you or has stopped loving you. You'll each find your way again.

Keep remembering (and telling her) how much you love her and how wonderful it is that your relationship has produced this miraculous baby.

Is Snoring Sexy?

The baby has been home a week. She's demanding your attention at all hours of the day and night. Both you and your partner have more work than you thought you could ever handle. Your hormones are fluctuating. You may be eating irregularly.

You are both exhausted.

Your partner (and lover) may be more interested in cuddling with the baby than fooling around with you.

Your soul mate is less buff than she was nine months ago. Or else she's on bed rest after her caesarean.

Your partner and her body have been through an intense ordeal. Remember when she screamed "look what you did to me!!!" during labor? She may still remind you occasionally how "*you* didn't give birth to this baby."

Ready to "set the mood" for foreplay?

Do not fear. You are normal, even if all of life's recent disruptions leave you horny, frustrated, out of synch, or all of the above.

Almost every new parent has to work at rekindling the romance and intimacy. Guys usually like a quick response when it "comes" to sex, but you may need a few new skills now.

The key is keeping a long-term perspective—long term as in more than the next two minutes, two days, or two weeks.

Back in Play

Fathering author Kevin Osborn says sex after childbirth is like getting back on the field after ACL rehab. Your partner is your intimacy all-star, but she may need her doctor (usually the OB/GYN) to sign off before she can return to practice. Your dynamic duo won't play every down at first. It may also take a few reps to get back in game condition.

One or both of you may be afraid of getting pregnant again so soon after the intense pregnancy, labor, delivery, and infant care scenario. If you both do want more children, you need to discuss how soon you want them.

DAD WORDS

Should women have children after 35? Thirty-five children is enough for any woman.

—Gracie Allen

There is no "normal" timetable for when and how your mutual sexual desire will return. It might come back with some new wrinkles and possibilities. Once it does, you still have to negotiate some new realities.

For example, the area inside your partner's vagina can be sore and/or dry for weeks or months, even after her other physical problems heal. Remember that this too shall pass—and that your drug store sells K-Y.

While You Wait

You both will probably crave physical touch and affection during any waiting period, if not always at the same moment. Make the extra effort to be affectionate—not in anticipation of getting some, but just to show your care and support. You'll be surprised by the benefits. She'll know that you care about her, still *want* to touch her, and value her for more than her booty. You'll experience a new level of intimacy, because your no-strings-attached care during the chaos brings you closer together.

You might need to practice this M.O. because she may not immediately recognize your affection as a random act of love. Your relationship's history may have taught her that any hug or kiss comes with a sexual agenda or expectation.

Finding your sexual rhythm may take some weeks or months, but hang in there and stay up ... as in upbeat. The other kind can't hurt, either.

Don't go cruising for someone else to "provide a little comfort" while you and mom regain your footing. That's an extremely radical reaction to a short-term problem. An emotional and/or physical affair with someone else is certainly no "solution" to your situation. It undermines the trust essential for a truly intimate relationship, deeply damages your connection (even if you don't get "caught"), and absolutely threatens your bond with your new baby. Plus, it's just dumb.

Fathering is a long-term commitment, lasting the rest of your life, no matter what temporary difficulties accompany your journey. The smart guys recognize how the same principles apply to a truly committed romantic relationship.

Remember all the different ways that intimacy flows through an intimate relationship. Use them all during this time of physical transition.

Sharing Her Breasts

A new dad won't suffer physical wounds from childbirth (unless mom really lost it during labor). But you may feel rejected, insecure, or abandoned if mom is depressed or not interested in sex. Because your issues may be nonphysical, they can be harder to nail down.

Many new dads wonder if sex will feel the same now. Will we fit together (literally and figuratively)? What do I say if I don't feel like doing it when she does? How will I react if I want to do it, and she doesn't? Will I still find her sexy ... and will she find me desirable? Are her breasts off limits now because the baby uses them? Will we ever be romantic or hot for each other again?

These worries, and others like them, are normal.

EXTRA POINT

Veteran dads who went before you really did survive childbirth's fallout; we lived to make love again. Remember, men usually don't stay deflated about sex for very long.

Just like everything else in fatherhood, remember that you can ask for help if your questions or problems persist. The question can be hard, but as my father used to say: If you never ask your question, the answer is always "No."

There is often major upside to post-birth sex. Many of us feel closer to our partners than ever before. We're awed by this miracle we're living through: a baby who is here because we had sex!

If you participate fully in your partner's pregnancy and your child's upbringing, a powerful and visceral connection will develop between you and your family.

Experiencing this sense of wonder together can bring you and your partner closer together than ever before. Such emotional, psychological, and spiritual intimacy is very fulfilling. It can also open new experiences of physical intimacy—which is very fun.

Fishing for Romance

As you know firsthand by now, "normal" has left the building. Many things at home and in life will never be the same. Amid all this change, it's essential to focus on continuing to nurture your relationship with your partner. As the old saying goes, a relationship is like a fish—it has to keep moving forward in order to live.

It can be hard to pay attention to your relationship—or to your partner—when there is so much baby care, housework, and job work to do. You may be spending lots of time in the same vicinity. But that's very different from spending time together.

Whatever you do, when your partner is quiet or just "plugging along," don't assume that everything is fine. She may have things on her mind or be feeling low, yet stay quiet because she doesn't want to burden you—or doesn't want to admit that motherhood is anything other than pure ecstasy.

So check in regularly. Ask how she's doing. And give her the gift of sharing how you're doing and what you're thinking. Tell her when you're feeling less than enthusiastic about sleep deprivation, cleaning up poop, and the other "joys" of parenting.

Even though you have a child, it's not too late to date your partner. Schedule a night or afternoon out together regularly. Sure, you may have to pay for a sitter, but that's a small outlay for investing in your most important relationship. Make the date its very own special event, rather than an appendage to something you're already doing. It doesn't have to be fancy—just be sure that you are alone together.

Try talking about something other than your baby. That strengthens your relationship and reminds you both that your lives include other important things.

The Least You Need to Know

- Prenatal sex can be awesome.
- Follow her OB/GYN's guidance on sex to avoid problems.
- Have fun experimenting with sexual positions and activities before and after childbirth.
- Patience and alternative forms of sexual intimacy will strengthen your relationship with mom.

The First Season

After a few weeks with your infant, you've figured out a few things and started to develop your routine. Routine is especially important for the baby, because he doesn't yet have vast intellectual capacity for making his own decisions. He's still trying to eat, sleep, and stay warm. (Pooping is his bonus.)

As his development accelerates, his needs—and his routine—will change. This is entirely normal, so don't take it personally.

In this last part of the book, you explore what's happening to your baby between now and his first birthday, and what those developments mean for you. I offer pointers about finding your strengths, responding to baby's new abilities, and securing your relationship with the baby and your parenting partner.

Plus, I clue you in about bedtime, playtime, teething, and more.

Finding the Sweet Spot

In This Chapter

- Bonding with baby
- Understanding routines and discipline
- Playing to learn

You may be a rookie dad, but that baby settled in at home is your All-Star. You have a million tasks to juggle, so your dad-baby rhythm will be better on some days than others. You may or may not feel as connected to him as you thought you would. You may even think the baby looks like a wrinkled old man and wonder if she'll ever be cute. That's okay!

The more involved you are, the more quickly you'll discover your own sweet spots—the areas where you excel at parenting.

ET, Phone ER

Admit it: newborns can look weird. Your baby's head is huge in proportion to the rest of her body. It may look more pointy than round after squeezing through the birth canal. Parts of her body might be covered with less-than-attractive vernix—a white grease that protects baby's skin inside the womb, and that can stick around for a while after birth. She may have rashes or splotchy-colored skin. Then there's that grotesque, dark purple umbilical cord stump!

She may not seem to resemble anyone on either side of your families—or anyone on the planet. Her shriveled-up fingers and toes might look like they've been soaked in water for months (well, they sort of have been). Intellectually, you know that baby isn't going to keep looking strange, but still ….

If you don't feel instantly overwhelmed with affection for this strange-looking creature, don't worry. Before long, you will know her well, and she won't look like Benjamin Button anymore.

Remember that nobody (including you) ever met this little person before—so even though you've been expecting her, she is a stranger.

If you survey honest parents, some will admit to having mixed feelings when encountering their first child. They had moments of uncertainty, discomfort, fear, confusion, aversion, queasiness, euphoria, affection, distance, panic, protectiveness, speechlessness, pride, terror, responsibility, awe, love, and more. So, if you feel any or all of these things, you're not alone. You haven't failed.

 DAD WORDS

We will be friends until forever, just you wait and see.

—Winnie the Pooh

Like most parts of fathering, the benefits come when you show up and do your part. The more time you spend feeding, burping, changing, and holding your baby, the more attached you'll feel to each other. You will connect.

Bonding Is Ensured

You'll need patience throughout your fathering journey. For example, it may take a while before your father-baby connection feels natural and easy. There will be times when holding the baby a certain way calms her on Thursday, but not on Friday. There will be times when you and your partner disagree about how to do something with the baby or around the house. All of these situations call for patience— even though patience is hard to maintain when you're under stress!

If you're feeling stressed about bonding with the baby, patience is extra important. Remember that doing bonding activities—even from a sense of obligation—will eventually lead to the bonding feelings you want.

Start with physical and verbal connection. An infant operates primarily on sensory stimulation. She cries for food because her stomach feels empty. She cries for a clean diaper because her butt feels sore. Rocking and singing calm her down because those sensations are similar to what she felt and heard for nine months in the uterus.

So right from the get-go, get in there and interact. In the hospital and during the following weeks, go out of your way to burp, change, feed, and rock the baby. Look into her eyes and talk to her. If any of this feels awkward or forced, don't sweat it, just keep doing it.

> **EXTRA POINT**
>
> Repeated physical contact ensures that you will grow to know your baby better, feel more confident and comfortable interacting with her, and build the powerful father-child bonds that you both need.

The baby will give you valuable feedback, too. Eventually, she will relax when you dab her tears, take her for a stroll, or rock her to sleep. When you see and feel the positive results of your involvement, your connection steadily strengthens.

A few dads feel absolute, instantaneous, and unyielding bonds with their infants. If that's you, three cheers! But don't worry if you have a few experiences that challenge the notion that what happens today with your child will remain the same forever. Keep building the bond in both the mundane and the unusual activities you share with your baby. That investment ensures that your bond will mature.

Routine Rotations

Baby needs a repeated pattern of activities to induce sleep, eating, and other essentials.

What's the big deal with routine? She can't survive without it.

Even if she's drinking a few ounces of milk at a time, your baby consumes far more nutrition (in proportion to her weight) than an adult does. She also pees and poops more. Completing all these tasks requires a lot of work on her part and yours.

Some babies adapt to a routine more easily than others, and nearly every baby will change her routine. Don't wait for advance warning or formal notification of these changes. Change is normal.

It Worked for Me!

It's also normal if your baby's routine doesn't emerge during her first few weeks. She's still adapting to life outside the womb—perhaps the most abrupt life adjustments she'll ever make. Even so, start looking for and working toward patterns that work.

Other parents' experience can be a big help as you develop workable baby routines. But not every trick in another parent's book will work for you.

For example, the usual solution my wife and I used on our twins to stop their colic-induced crying was walking and rocking them. But when that method would fail, one or both of us put the girls in their car seats and took them for a ride. The movement of the car always settled them down and eventually they'd fall asleep. The challenge was getting them to drop off before we were arrested for DWD: dozing while driving.

Many parents find that the car seat solution cures uncontrollable crying or an over-tired baby. But Brook and his wife just couldn't get it to work for their son. Friends gave Brook all kinds of additional advice: play only country music, drive on the interstate, drive on back roads, only drive at night. "It didn't matter," Brook says, "he cried for a year. This wasn't supposed to be how it went! Why didn't driving the baby around work for us?"

Then, one day, an Indigo Girls song, "The Power of Two," came on the car radio. The baby stopped crying immediately and looked peacefully out the window at the sky. The parents noticed, and took full advantage.

"Once we drove to Nashville from Indianapolis," Brook says, "and we listened to that song repeatedly for hours, just to get my son to sleep. If he woke up and the song wasn't playing, he would start crying again until we put it back on. He had us well trained!"

Eventually, "Sunshine on My Shoulders" by John Denver produced a similar effect for Brook's son—and gave the parents one additional tune to run on endless loop in their brains.

 DAD WORDS

I didn't hesitate to kiss my father in public. And that's how I tried to raise my children. We're physical.

—Payne Stewart

The lesson: welcome other parents' suggestions—and be prepared to adapt their strategies (or create your own) to make your routines work well. And remember that routine requires a level of repetition that may make your head explode.

Shhhhh! Baby's in the House

Back in Chapter 2, I talk about creating safe and quiet spaces for the baby in your home. Now that the baby has arrived, you'll see if your arrangements are working out as planned. Can the baby sleep undisturbed by noise from the kitchen while you make lunch or dinner? Does the streetlight's glare through that crack in the curtain trigger a crying episode? What time does your neighbor in 2B start the blender for her morning smoothie? These questions become very important while establishing your regular home routine.

So keep your eyes open for ways to make your physical setup more conducive to your baby care needs. Changing things around doesn't mean you screwed up when you arranged the nursery; it means you're adapting to realities that are impossible to anticipate before the baby is born.

You may need to change some of your personal habits around the house, too. You'll need to relocate loud phone calls, arguments, and impromptu *American Idol* face-offs to the backyard. You might need headphones to contain the sound from your stereo, computer, or tablet. You'll also have to establish limits for visitors so that their enthusiasm doesn't do too much to disturb the baby's sleep or disrupt your routine.

Knowing the Score

Your baby will provide the data you need to begin building his routine. He already knows how to cry and fuss when he's tired, hungry, wet, or wants your attention. You'll naturally start reading the subtleties in his cues.

If you observe and listen closely, you'll begin to sense the differences between his hungry and tired cries. Compare notes with your partner to get her interpretation. If you feed him to stop his crying, but he doesn't seem interested in eating—that's evidence that the cry was about being tired or poopy instead. You'll catch on if you're paying attention. Parental instinct helps a lot with this, so trust your gut!

HEADS UP

If your "regular" ways to comfort baby don't work, he might be catching a cold, getting a fever, or starting to teethe. Consult with your pediatrician, and you'll soon be able to sense such problems as they occur.

Your next step: start taking notes. You and your partner can write down the times of day that he's hungry, playful, laid back, and tired. Track the length of time between when he eats and when he poops. Get a sense of how long four ounces of milk will hold him until he wants to eat again.

Don't look for pinpoint accuracy—babies don't have it. Use your notes to get a general idea about the natural pattern his body is following.

This information gives you a foundation to build routine on. It helps you to anticipate when he's ready for food, play, or a nap. You want to take advantage of his "schedule" of needs so you can reinforce them into a routine.

Build your routine (and your expectations) around key moments of the baby's day. For example, if he goes down for "the night" around 6 P.M., plan to have dinner around 4. Yes, that may sound crazy, but baby sets much of your agenda for the first year, so get used to it. If it's July, he may go down at 6 and wake for his first "night" feeding while the sun is still up. If that's frustrating, be grateful you're not raising the kid in Lapland, where the July sun never sets.

Working backward from bedtime and dinner, you can determine good times for other feedings, his afternoon nap, his morning nap, your own meals, and other routine activities. You can also capitalize on his playful and alert patterns. Those are the best times of day to invite grandparents over for a visit (or take him over to their house).

HEADS UP

Flexibility is essential. As your baby grows, his physical and sensory development continues to accelerate. His natural "schedule" will change as his needs change. This means you will have to adjust—and sometimes revamp—the routine. This is normal and healthy, even if maddening. Roll with it.

Of course, you have personal needs that must be met as part of your new family's routine. Most parents eventually return to work, often at workplaces that can't (or won't) adjust their schedules to a baby's schedule. If that's the case, *you* have to adjust.

Before your back-to-work date, start establishing a routine designed to get baby to day care and you to your job on time. Always include wiggle room, even if it intrudes on your sleep. Need to leave for work by 7? Aim to have your morning baby routine completed by 6:30.

Start waking and feeding the baby at a regular time (in this scenario, around 5:30), so you and he get used to the schedule. Allow plenty of time for changing his diapers, dressing him for the outside weather, and securing him in the car seat. Oh, and brushing your teeth, too. Several "dry runs" may be necessary to get it all figured out, so don't wait until the morning of your first day to do it for the first time.

Be patient and relax. If things don't go smoothly, that doesn't mean the baby is out to get you. It means you have more work to do.

Think about housebreaking a puppy (and don't tell your partner that I made another dog training reference). After days of success, the puppy may pee on the kitchen floor and eagerly wag her tail, as if to say: "See, I peed just like you wanted me to!" The dog doesn't know any better and hasn't learned the important (to you) difference between the lawn and the floor.

A dog's brain can weigh less than an avocado—and have the same level of intelligence—so canines "mature" faster than humans. Conclusion: babies are exponentially more difficult to "train" than dogs. Don't expect you and Junior to develop a daily routine as quickly and easily as you and Rover did. Take the patience you need to train a dog and then multiply by 1,000. If your child's name is Rover, then you're on your own.

When to Call the Doctor

New parents are very concerned about the health of their infants—and usually lack the experience to know how sick is "too" sick. You may feel the urge to call your pediatrician's office twice a day. Or you may feel too embarrassed to call at all. All of these reactions are normal for first-time dads and moms.

Ask your pediatrician for guidance about when to reach out for advice, or bring the baby in for medical attention. It's a very good idea to get medical expertise if your baby …

- Becomes sluggish or inactive.
- Will not eat.
- Cries more than usual.
- Develops an unusual rash (something other than a heat or diaper rash).
- Has a fever of more than 100 degrees Fahrenheit or 37.7 Celsius.
- Vomits repeatedly (not just spitting up).
- Has frequent loose, watery bowels.
- Is breathing rapidly, wheezing, or having any difficulty in breathing.

- Has Apnea episodes (times when baby stops breathing for long periods).
- Has any kind of skin infection, including at the site of a circumcision.

Before your call your physician or nurse practitioner, write down your child's symptoms. Take your child's temperature. Have your pharmacy's phone number on hand to tell the doctor. Keep a notepad handy to write down any instructions. And don't hang up until you have all of your questions answered.

Disciples of Discipline

Thoughts of training lead naturally to thoughts about discipline. Despite what many people think, discipline isn't punishment—at least effective discipline isn't.

Discipline is one of those words that come to English from Latin, in this case, the Latin word *disciplina*, which means instruction given to a student. The same root gives us the word *disciple*—someone who follows a mentor or teacher.

Start now to think of discipline as guiding and teaching, rather than as punishing. You can't reasonably punish an infant anyway, since he isn't capable (yet) of willfully disobeying you. Guide your child toward the positive ends you want, rewarding him with encouragement—rather than treats or other prizes—when he goes in that positive direction.

Infant Morality

Caring for an infant can be incredibly frustrating. The baby fusses, cries, and simply won't go to sleep when you want him to. You're trying to get him ready for day care or a visit to Aunt Millie's, and he simply won't eat. You're flying to Phoenix tomorrow morning to introduce the baby to his grandparents, and he develops a fever.

Is this baby out to get you?!?

No. He'd need free will, forethought, and intention to inflict pain on you consciously. He will have those characteristics in abundance in about 15 years, but not today.

Infants don't have what it takes to punish you, so don't punish your infant—under any circumstances.

As I discuss in later chapters, it takes your baby a while before he can even fully differentiate between mom and dad. His thinking isn't very sophisticated. Starting out, his still-developing brain is in survival mode. He is reacting to basic, internal stimuli like hunger, tiredness, alertness, feeling cold, and feeling wet.

Recent research suggests that infants respond best to those who offer them help—and that infants tend to offer their own kind of help and comfort to others. Infants also tend to have more positive reactions to other people (and puppets) who act and eat like them. Researchers such as Yale professor Dr. Karen Wyn argue that these findings demonstrate that morality begins in infancy. Of course, others argue that everything depends on how you define morality.

For your purposes (and sanity) as a dad, consider this:

- There is no evidence that babies act "immorally" or with malice.
- Infants respond to help, comfort, and familiarity—and seem to offer help and comfort in return.
- These patterns of response contribute directly to the infant's survival and thriving, by facilitating bonds with his parents and other potentially nurturing adults.
- It runs completely counter to the human survival instinct for a baby to drive his parent(s) away.

So, if your baby is out to get you anywhere, he's out to get you closer to him. His fingernail-on-the-chalkboard screams are expressions of pain, hunger, or exhaustion. They aren't expressions of spite (or anything else) toward you.

When you feel frustrated by your infants' behavior, and/or your ability to calm and comfort him, don't blame the baby or try to change anything about him (except his diaper).

Instead, focus on what you can do for yourself. Here are some examples of things you can do to regain your equilibrium:

- Take a deep breath.
- Lay the baby down in a safe place and leave the room for a moment to calm yourself.
- Call a friend or relative to vent your frustration; if they've had infants, they'll understand.
- Remember what he is and isn't capable of.

Loving's the Limit

Ask a parent why he's disciplining his child, and he's likely to answer, "I don't want her to get hurt." Your baby (and children of all ages) need you to provide safety, direction, stimulation, support, affection, acceptance, challenge, loyalty, and other valuable things.

The best ways to keep your baby safe are childproofing your home and being alert when driving, carrying, and changing her.

As she gets older and more mobile, her safety requires you to begin introducing the most basic elements of discipline: saying "No" ("No thank you" works well, too) and distracting the baby away from dust bunnies and other dangers.

Be firm, but gentle in guiding her away from dangerous things (like sucking on electrical cords). Yelling isn't necessary or very productive. Saying "no" isn't enough on its own. You must also offer more interesting alternatives, like time playing or reading with you. Eventually, babies (and especially toddlers) make "no" into a game. They love playing it, testing you and teasing you. The No game has that extra benefit of teaching them your limits.

> **DAD WORDS**
>
> My dad was really into [being a dad], so just by osmosis, I'm just really into it. I never really looked at it as a chore or whatever. When I hear people talk about juggling, or the sacrifices they make for their children, I look at them like they're crazy, because "sacrifice" infers that there was something better to do than being with your children. And I've never been with my kids and gone, "Man, I wish I was on my stage right now." Being with my kids is the best, most fun thing. It's a privilege. It's not something I call a sacrifice.
>
> —Chris Rock

During the baby's first year, it's especially helpful to focus on fun when establishing limits and routines. Your child will have more good times than bad times, so be sure to build on that. Years of research consistently demonstrate the most effective way to discipline and raise a responsible child is to "catch" him being good.

The urge to punish is understandable, but it's an urge you need to resist during year one. Revenge is irrelevant with a baby. Why? It doesn't work to impose negative outcomes on a human being who isn't developed enough to understand them. So dismiss "punish" from your vocabulary for a while.

Think of your role as training and guiding. As she gets older, she'll have the capacity to respond consciously when you train her mind and moral character. For now, and in the future, remember how important her mistakes are in this process. Mistakes hurt, but there are certain things you can't learn (such as walking and speaking) without making mistakes. Her mistakes are outstanding opportunities for you to step in with your direction, stimulation, support, affection, acceptance, challenge, and loyalty.

Learning and limits are essential elements of love. Think of a hug, which is 1) a wonderful way to express love, and 2) a great metaphor for loving relationships. A hug has natural limits; you can't be outside of someone's arms and inside her hug. When engaged in a loving hug, you don't want to be someplace else—so you don't attempt to leave.

Good hugs also require a degree of negotiation. I have reading glasses hanging down from a strap around my neck. I often forget that the glasses are there, even when hugging one of my daughters. Although now adults, my girls are still short—my glasses poke them right in the ear or face during a hug, so I have to move them out of the way (usually after they remind me to move them). Otherwise, the hug hurts.

Try thinking of hugs as your metaphor for discipline. Effective discipline is loving, it has limits, and it works best when you adjust for circumstances you may or may not recognize right away.

Playing Games

Among the many responsibilities accompanying your baby's first year is the fatherly responsibility to play! Your child's healthy development depends on playful interaction with you, other adults, and your surroundings. The key word is interaction.

That means avoiding play or toys that require electricity. For example, research shows that exposure to television and other stimuli delivered by screens hampers a baby's brain development and can lead to higher levels of anxiety, aggression, and attention deficits later on.

That's why the American Academy of Pediatrics strongly recommends (and has for years) *no* screen time for children under age two. That's no as in zero. The "educational" claims of video products like *Your Baby Can Read* and *Baby Einstein* have been debunked, with lawsuits forcing some companies to issue refunds to parents.

To actually stimulate your baby's intellectual—and social— development, you and your partner are the most essential educational "toy." Gives new meaning to the idea of toys are us, doesn't it?

During infancy, your play can take many forms; here are some ideas:

- Talk and sing to her in normal and goofy voices
- Respond to her noises and facial expressions

- Let her grab your finger
- Gently move her limbs about
- Make faces and funny noises
- Wiggle her toes
- Gently swing her around in the air or in your arms

This is the kind of stimulation her brain and body needs most in the early weeks and months.

Play is how babies learn, so playtime doesn't have to be time for you to instruct your child. Instead, follow her lead and her curiosity. In most cases, her innate playful instincts will provide her with thousands of opportunities to learn how to interact with people, manipulate objects, walk, talk, and develop many other skills. You don't need lesson plans!

Dad: No Batteries Needed

As I mention in Chapter 1, research shows that a father's tendency to be more at ease with physicality is a huge asset for his children. Dads are more likely to hold babies facing outward—observing, interacting with, and enjoying the larger world.

A dad is more likely than a mom to bounce a baby on his knee or twirl her around in the air like a plane. As kids get older, dads are more likely to tickle, wrestle, and roughhouse with kids. They're more likely to encourage, support, and challenge their kids to take physical, emotional, and intellectual risks.

Of course, dads are not alone in these physical interactions—many moms do these things, too. And like each of our talents, we have to be smart about our physicality; for example, not being so rough that you harm the baby.

Over time, researchers say, your interactive play with your baby and child will help her have the following results:

- More secure attachment
- More emotional flexibility and resilience

- Less gender role stereotyping
- More generosity and awareness of other people's needs
- Higher tolerance for frustration
- Less impulsivity

Stack those accomplishments up against any TV show or iPad app, and you win.

READING THE SIGNS

According to Campaign for a Commercial-Free Childhood: Hands-on play is essential to children's health and well-being. Play is the foundation of learning and creativity. Play promotes critical thinking, self-regulation, and constructive problem solving as children explore, experiment, and initiate—rather than merely react. Children play to express their feelings, gain a sense of competence, and make meaning of their experience.

Toy Talk

Children play naturally. Your baby will begin playing as his eyesight, hearing, and dexterity improve, usually between one and three months old. This sensory development helps him tell the difference between sounds and sights—mostly the sounds and sights of you and your partner. Before long, he'll grab your finger, surprising you with his strength. Then, he'll learn to close his hand into a fist. That helps him learn to hold a rattle. After he uses the rattle for a while, he'll begin to realize that he's the one generating the rattle's noise.

Because play develops so naturally, from a very early age, you'd think play is a simple, straightforward aspect of parenting and childhood. Turns out, there are volumes of academic and scientific research on play. Some parenting authors translate that research into plain English and include it in mainstream books.

As a parent, your biggest play issue may be marketing of "educational" materials and toys. People in the United States buy about

$22 billion worth of toys every year, up from $17 billion in 1992. That's a dramatic increase given the decline in birthrates over that same period. There are more varieties of toys—and more sophisticated methods of marketing them—than ever before.

Child development specialists debate whether a greater variety of toys is good for kids, but the toy industry's growth trend isn't much use to you or your baby. The reason is simple. Babies only need the simplest of toys to play with.

As soon as he can sit up, your baby will want to play with a ball. So all he needs is a round object that 1) rolls, and 2) he can't swallow. A ball that lights up, talks, or dials your cellphone is completely unnecessary—and some emerging research indicates that this kind of electronic stimulation can harm a baby's brain development, just as screen time can.

Simple toys (like a plain old ball) leave openings for your baby's developing brain to fill in the blanks. Rather than being distracted by lights and noise, he focuses on understanding why the ball rolls the way it does, how your actions influence the path of the ball, how his actions influence it, the joy of making something outside of himself move, the joy of seeing your excitement about his developing skills, and so on.

Creative play is essential for the healthy development of your baby's brain and social skills. Too many new toys preempt the child's initiative and creativity with artificial stimulation—which many toy manufacturers claim is educational.

Before anything else, babies (and older children) need stimulation from other human beings and from their own brains and senses. During his first year, your child (and you) will get the most benefit and enjoyment from toys like these:

- Rattles
- Balls
- Blocks
- Cups, plates, utensils
- Natural noisemakers (like a metal pie plate)

- Stuffed animals and dolls (labeled as safe for 12 months and under)
- Board books (that you can read aloud and he can chew)

Most babies have an incredible capacity to learn. Your baby needs (and wants) to learn about the people and environment nearby. He can play in unique ways, discover what he finds interesting, and learn what is special about himself. He has an innate sense of wonder with a hunger to solve problems and a desire to explore.

DAD WORDS

Play is often talked about as if it were a relief from serious learning. But for children, play is serious learning. Play is really the work of childhood.

—Fred Rogers

For you and your baby, play is simultaneously fun and healthy. Play as often as possible.

The Least You Need to Know

- Routines are essential for the baby; and she will change them.
- Parental interaction is the most valuable and fun kind of play.
- Your baby needs guidance, not punishment; she's not out to get you.

Game Changers: Nontraditional Fatherhood

In This Chapter

- Managing your other important relationships
- Fathering from afar
- Embracing nontraditional fatherhood
- Staying involved, even when it's difficult

Consider women under 30 giving birth in the United States. More than half of them aren't married when they have their children. It's hard to find statistics on the relationship status of these babies' fathers but, for now, let's assume that most of them are unmarried, too.

Some unmarried parents consciously plan their pregnancies as part of what they hope to be a long-term, committed, intimate partnership. A small percentage of pregnancies result from a one-night stand. Married people also have unplanned pregnancies. Other unplanned pregnancies happen to parents in a short-term relationship, which may or may not end before the baby is born. Other adults plan their pregnancies with the intention of raising their children alone.

Most laws and customs in the United States and Canada operate with the assumption that a baby's parents are heterosexuals who are married to each other. On a practical level, this means that married heterosexual parents have the least legal and social hassles when they become parents. For example, if your wife has a child, you don't need to prove your paternity—if your name is on the birth certificate, the law presumes that you're the father because you're married to the mother. The law puts more hurdles in front of unmarried fathers trying to establish their place in their children's life—and some jurisdictions make it virtually impossible for gay couples.

Leaving the courthouse and returning to the nursery, an infant doesn't give a rat's posterior about his parents' marital, sexual, racial, immigration, ethical, or economic status. He's completely dependent on his parents for survival. As the child gets older, his parents continue to have major influence in his life. For the first 15 to 30 years, no one will have more impact.

In this chapter I offer advice for nontraditional dads. Just because you didn't follow a traditional path to fatherhood doesn't mean that you can't have a robust, fulfilling, and nurturing relationship with your child.

ESP and Co-Parenting

It's obvious by now that I'm a big fan of dads handling as many parenting duties as possible. Those everyday activities build your relationships with your children and family.

Guys like to measure things and have concrete evidence about what's happening. In recent years, parents and advocates developed the ideas of equally shared parenting (ESP), along with tools to help you figure out how you're dividing up your obligations and opportunities for child-rearing, career, self-care, and other important things.

ESP is a concept developed by forward-thinking parents like Marc and Amy Vachon, authors of the book *Equally Shared Parenting* (equallysharedparenting.com). The Vachons describe a way of dividing home, relationship, and work duties equally between parents. Ideally, this prevents either adult from feeling shortchanged or like they are the "other" parent.

ESP starts from the belief that both dad and mom need to suit up and show up for responsible parenting, because the involvement of both parents helps the child. Shared parenting requires clear communication, so both of you know your joint and individual goals, styles, and strengths.

Few of us were taught the skills needed to work successfully with someone else to raise a child. But the payoff is huge, as demonstrated by the following facts:

- Your kids will do better and be happier when they have the love and support of both parents (even if it's from two different homes).
- Your kids need to see you talk respectfully with the other parent. Remember—that's their mom or dad you're talking to and they love that parent!
- Regular communication can help keep little parenting misunderstandings from becoming big conflicts.

Because she is so dependent, your infant is rapidly forming attachments. It's essential that you are with her consistently so that she can attach to you. Even at this very young age, you and mom need to minimize changes and disruptions in the baby's life, while giving her love and affection. Without reliable attachment, the baby may develop problems with feeding, sleeping, and excessive crying.

Creating a Parenting Plan

If you and mom are not living together, you need a plan for parenting. A good plan has two requirements: 1) you write it down, and 2) you follow it.

If you end up in family mediation or family court, you may get a legal order laying out your respective parenting responsibilities. You will still be better off if you supplement the legal stuff with a day-to-day life plan that you agree on together.

EXTRA POINT

If the emotions of breaking up are still too intense, ask a dispassionate third party (like a mediator) to help you create your co-parenting plan.

Raising a baby requires many daily duties and decisions. Start your plan by coming up with a list of these responsibilities. Then—remembering that your top priority is what's best for your child—make a plan for how you two will make particular decisions related to the child you created together.

Take medical care as an example. Who will decide whether the baby needs to see a doctor? Just one of you? Both of you in consultation with each other? Whichever parent the baby is with at the moment? What happens if it's an emergency and/or one parent can't reach the other one? What expectations do you have about informing one another about the baby's medical care?

You can use these questions (and others like them) on a whole range of topics, such as these:

- Child care
- Grandparent and extended family visits
- Holidays and birthdays
- Legal decisions affecting the child
- Traveling with the child (especially across state and national borders)

You can find templates and guidelines for co-parenting plans online, for example: www.nolo.com/legal-encyclopedia/parenting-agreements-29565.html.

Once again, these are valuable issues to work through even if you and mom are married and/or still living together. More plan-ahead communication is almost always better.

Gay Dads

Gay fathers don't have as many legal protections as nongay fathers. A gay dad has a hard time getting insurance and other employment-related benefits for his child if she isn't his biological child. Even in adoption, some states recognize only one adult in a gay couple as the adoptive parent, leaving the other parent without legal standing. In other states, both fathers can petition for a joint adoption.

Under the law, the "legally recognized" dad is the only one allowed to decide on the health, education, and well-being of the couple's children. In many states, if the "legally recognized" father dies or is incapacitated, a member of his family will have the right to become the legal guardian for the child … but his partner may not.

Without the legal presumption that both fathers are legal parents, it's crucial to have written agreements about what you want to happen with your child. Obviously, you need a clearly articulated will (see gaywill.com/faq.php) for the worst situations, but you also need documents that deal with everyday situations (e.g., giving your partner "permission" to make medical decisions for the baby if he's the one in the emergency room).

A good resource is Lambda Legal, a national nonprofit that uses litigation, education, and public policy to gain legal and civil rights for lesbians, gay men, bisexuals, the transgendered, and people with HIV or AIDS. Call 212-809-8585 or visit lambdalegal.org. State laws, state courts, and federal courts regularly move to permit or prohibit some aspect of gay rights. Check Lambda Legal or Nolo Publishing (nolo.com/legal-encyclopedia/lgbt-law) for the latest in what laws and rulings determine policy where you live.

Teen Dads

Many people write off teen fathers as irresponsible and incapable of being a positive force in their children's lives. If you decide (as you should) to defy that stereotype, it won't be easy—and you won't be alone.

According to research by Child Trends (www.childtrends.org), about two-thirds of teen fathers in the United States are 18 or 19—already adults. Nearly all of these young men are born in the United States; 48 percent are white, 29 percent black, and 19 percent Hispanic. And contrary to popular belief, the rate of teen pregnancy has been trending downward for several years.

The biggest challenge for a teen dad is relationship status. Most teen fathers are live-away dads. Less than half live with the mom when baby is born, and fewer than 1 in 10 are married.

Teen dads have more difficulty finding jobs that pay enough to support a family—or even live independently. The same is true for teen moms. As a result, many teen parents remain living with their own parents. So a common scenario looks like this:

Dad goes to visit his baby. He leaves his parents' home and arrives at the home of his child's other grandparents, where the baby's mother (who may or may not still be his romantic partner) lives. This isn't his turf. Mom and her parents may be hovering around, judging and critiquing his interaction with the baby. They may look down on him for not doing more for the baby and for mom. They may express resentment that dad isn't still involved with mom, and that he "got" her pregnant. He may act defensive and critical in return, his focus distracted from the baby.

Or, he may take the baby back to his parents' home for a visit, where he may run into judgment, critique, and resentment from his own parents!

Of course, many grandparents are very supportive of their sons and daughters if they become teen parents. And most teen parents still are (and plan to remain) in a relationship with mom when the child is born. If dad and mom are cohabitating or married when baby comes, it markedly increases the odds that they will still be together five years later.

Other teen dads make the relationships with their children work. You're no slacker, so you can, too.

The key for you as a teen dad: don't let the difficulties get you down. Keep working, showing up, and doing more than your fair share. It won't be easy, and you will need to ask for help. But the more you're involved, and the more experience you gain, the easier your fathering life will become.

READING THE SIGNS

Your infant doesn't care how old his parents are or how much money you have. He cares only that you both are there for him consistently and love him without fail.

You might find it hard to have a long view of life while still young, but your child will help you. He is wonderful, living evidence of the legacy you will leave. A man is never too young to think about his legacy. With commitment and determination, you can do what needs to be done for your full involvement in your child's life and well-being.

Middle-Age Dads

There are two kinds of middle-age fathers. One is a Latin-speaking priest you'll find in *The Complete Idiot's Guide to the Middle Ages* (available from your favorite bookseller!). The other kind—men fathering children after 40—get our attention here.

Older dads and teen dads both encounter "that's not right" attitudes in our society. Some people think it's creepy or weird for a guy in his 40s, 50s, or older to have a child. Let's repeat, all together now, "Bull."

First-time fathers older than 40 are entirely capable of being good dads. Research even suggests that they are more likely than the average dad to take responsibility for a young child. It is more likely for them to intend to become a father, rather than contribute to an accidental pregnancy.

If you're a middle-age dad, your path shares some similarities with a teen dad. Don't let the stereotypes get you down. If strangers, friends, or family express Neanderthal notions like "you're too old for this," let it roll off your back. Tell them David Letterman had his first child in his fifties. (Other after-40 dads include Tony Blair, Mick Jagger, Paul McCartney, Jack Nicholson, and—post-60—Larry King.)

Older fathers are more likely to have resources, like a steady income and their own home. That can give you greater flexibility to be deeply involved in raising your infant. Not to mention the flexibility your baby will bring to your life!

My friend Dean and his wife loved parenting. He was around 50 when the last of their biological kids left home. So, they adopted two babies! I asked Dean how he had the energy to start over again, and he said: "I am astounded every day at how much energy they give me, and how flexible they keep me both physically and mentally."

There's no reason that you can't be a fabulous dad just because your age is higher than average for a first-time dad. Your baby won't start calling you "old man" until he's a teenager anyway.

Live-Away Dads

Most of our culture still assumes that mom is (and ought to be) the primary parent. That belief impacts dads in many ways—most dramatically when parents break up. For example, after a divorce, the odds are good that you will not be the parent who lives every day with your children. Family court may acknowledge you as a "non-custodial" father, a term I despise because it makes the kid sound like a commodity or piece of property. I prefer the more accurate, and less loaded, term "live-away" dad.

Psychologist and fathering expert William C. Klatte, LCSW, MSW, says a live-away dad knows he is succeeding when he remains a key part of his children's lives even when they aren't a part of his home. In *Live-Away Dads* (Penguin, 1999), Klatte writes that a father does this by making the kids his first priority, behaving responsibly himself, and not getting into power struggles with his ex.

DAD WORDS

I used to jump into pissing matches with my ex. Then I realized that my kid was always stuck in the middle of those pissing matches, getting wet and stinky. Once I stopped trying to one-up my ex, the tension almost disappeared. It takes two to fight; if I don't play, the "fight" peters out quickly.

—Barry

After years spent as a divorced father and social worker in family courts, Klatte suggests these tips for keeping the father-child bond strong, even when you don't live with your child:

- **Hang in there for the long haul.** Your involvement in your child's life may be different from your dreams for the two of you, but it is no less important. You remain a tremendous influence in her life and need to stay involved in a calm, loving, and committed way forever.

- **Develop healthy social and emotional supports for yourself.** Some live-away dads struggle to handle anger and loneliness with maturity. These feelings are normal, but be careful not to become emotionally dependent on your child. Instead, spend time with healthy adults and get your emotional and social needs met through them.

- **Remember that your child lives in two homes.** He may sometimes be upset, moody, or grieving when he leaves your home or your ex's home. Remember that your relationship with him is much more important than getting him to do things the way you think he should.

- **Father the best you can when she is with you.** You can't change how her other parent(s) raise her or make up for what they do or don't do. You can't correct their excessive leniency with your excessive strictness. Instead, father calmly. Be a patient and loving father, not a demanding and critical perfectionist. Be the dad she can always trust.

- **Keep your child out of the middle—even if your ex doesn't.** Talk well about his mother even when you're angry at her—and even if she talks poorly about you. Negative talk about your child's mother gives him a little wound, and causes him to think less of himself, his mom, and you. Resolve adult conflicts away from your child and allow him to be the child.

- **Don't misdirect anger at your ex toward your child.** When your child misbehaves, be careful not to confuse that behavior with her mother's actions, and instead, see what you can do to make things better.

- **Give your child consistent time and attention.** He needs your healthy attention in person, on the phone, over the internet, through the mail, or any other way. Don't try to buy his love with things, even if his mother does. Your child needs your presence, not your presents.

- **Listen to your child.** Accept her for who she is; not who you want her to be, think she should be, or think she would be if she were raised only by you. Take the lead in communicating, even when you feel unappreciated. You may not agree with everything she does or says (once she starts talking), but when you listen, you build the emotional connection that will help her listen to you when it really counts.

- **Focus on your child's positives.** Many men were raised by fathers pointing out what we did wrong, so we could fix it. That may work on the job, but not in the job of being a father. Focusing on negatives undermines your child's strength and confidence that are already stretched by living in two homes.

- **Be her father, not her mother.** You are a powerful and encouraging role model; show your child that she has a special place in your heart. Your masculine actions and loving words can help her realize that she, too, can be adventurous, playful, and successful, and should expect respect from other honorable men.

Most of these tips are good practice for the live-with dad as well. Be there, be loyal, be a role model, keep your word, nurture the child, respect your child, respect her mother, do your part—you get the idea.

Insuring Your Baby

If you and your partner aren't married, check right away to see if your health insurance carrier covers your baby's health-care costs. Some insurance companies may not. Coverage depends on how the insurer and/or your state's laws define terms like household, family, domestic partnership, and spouse; you don't automatically get the same presumption of rights with regard to your family as a married man does. That may not be fair, but it is true.

HEADS UP

Tell your insurance providers when new members join your family. Otherwise, you could run into problems with the baby's coverage. Check with your insurer about how soon after the birth you have to let them know.

At the same time, make sure that you and your partner work together to make health care decisions for the baby. You can save yourself a lot of trouble if—before the baby is born— you discuss the process you'll use to make decisions. If your baby gets sick, you'll have enough stress already.

Some other practical tasks for the unmarried dad:

- Update your life insurance and your will to list your new child as a beneficiary.
- If you don't have life insurance, consider getting some.
- If you don't have a will yet, get a move on!

Many websites offer free templates for making a will. Your will doesn't have to be complicated, but without one, some court will decide what to do with your assets, you won't have a say, and that will suck for your kid.

Most important, be an involved and engaged father. If your relationship with your partner should ever end, you will have to work out many of the same issues that a divorcing married couple does. When deciding custody questions, family court officials look closely at who has been caring for a kid. A judge will want to know who makes the child's doctor's appointments, arranges her birthday parties, attends school conferences, and the like.

If you don't know details about your child's medical conditions, medications, allergies, schedule, friends, and so on, a judge will view you as being somewhat indifferent to the child. In other words, there can be big legal implications later for how tuned in and engaged you are in your child's life now. Of course, the real reason to do and know this stuff about your kid is that it's good for you and your kid. And that's why society—including the courts—puts so much weight on it.

Tackling Touch Taboos

The last few decades have seen a steady rise in the number of fathers actively involved in raising their children. You'd think that might eliminate suspicion of dads who spend a lot of time with their kids. But it doesn't. Old attitudes die hard, and stories of fathers abusing their kids don't help.

Responsible fathers are furious and disgusted by the incidence of child sexual abuse, but we can struggle to sort out how our own fathering is impacted by other people's behaviors and attitudes.

In my book *Dads & Daughters*, I called this problem "the touch taboo." You may worry that others think it's wrong for you to be involved and affectionate with your baby. However, we actually harm our children if, for example, we let the prevalence of sexual abuse make us afraid to touch them, or afraid of how our healthy physical affection will be interpreted.

If good touch is absent from your relationship with your child, then you cut off part of who you and your child are. Babies (and parents) are tactile beings who need physical expressions of affection, comfort, reassurance, and playfulness. Words are not enough to convey the depth and importance of your love for your infant. Yet fear of being abusive—or perceived as being abusive—may stop you in your tracks.

DAD WORDS

I wanted to take up music, so my father bought me a blunt instrument. He told me to knock myself out.

—Jay London

My dad helped me immensely with affection. Like every other father or stepfather, his parenting was a mixed bag. He had plenty of problems, but almost every day, he hugged and kissed us kids—told us he loved us. He was affectionate with my many cousins as well. As far as I could tell, he hugged me as often he did my sisters—no gender discrimination.

He gave me a great legacy: the ability to be comfortable with, and draw comfort from, being physically affectionate with my kids.

Of course, not every father relates to his or other children this way. But no matter what your style of fathering, your child needs physical acknowledgement of your love for them now, and for years to come. That's sometimes not simple or easy to do, especially since few of us got clear lessons on the difference between good touch from bad touch while we were growing up. (Chapter 13 has more about how to discuss good touch/bad touch with your toddler.)

Identifying Good Touch

What is good touch? Touch is good when it does the following for your child:

- Comforts her
- Affirms her as a person
- Supports her
- Respects and is sensitive to her person and her boundaries
- Is given with her permission
- Is given freely, with no quid pro quo
- Helps her feel strong, lovable, and able to delight in herself
- Isn't sexual

Good touch goes beyond fatherly hugs and kisses. Good touch happens when you play with your infant, bouncing him, tickling him, loading him into and out of his car seat, and so on. As your child grows, good touch shows up when you play catch, garden, do carpentry, take dance lessons, train the dog, wrestle, shoot baskets, go for a walk, or do any number of things.

Plugging In to Tune In

My physical contact with my daughters began on their first day and enhanced one of nature's great miracles—a parent's ability to pick up signals for what their newborns need. The more I hugged, cuddled, and touched my premature infants, the better I got at recognizing those cues. This good touch also provided the most wonderful physical sensation of my life: having one of my infant daughters drop off to sleep on my shoulder, relaxing so completely that she seemed to melt into the indentation between my arm and chest.

As empathetic as I can be, I'll never fully know (as my wife likes to remind me) what it is like to feel another life living inside me for many months, or to experience the pain and euphoria of giving birth. As close as I can come is this baby melting on my chest and into my heart.

So throw all of yourself—your brain, heart, hands, and humor—into fathering your new baby. The rewards are amazing.

You may still have to take extra steps to show day care centers, schools, and doctors that you are, indeed, the parent primarily responsible for your child, especially if you're a single dad. That won't seem fair, but be direct, polite, and firm in asserting your responsibility and staying actively engaged in your child's life and activities.

The Least You Need to Know

- You can share parenting, no matter where you live.
- If you're unmarried, take extra steps to ensure your place in the baby's life.
- You will succeed as a dad by working on what's best for your child.
- Teach your child the difference between good touch and bad touch.

Off and Running: Months Two to Six

In This Chapter

- Keeping up with baby's early development
- Dealing with the changes
- Being good at fathering
- Embracing the fun

Had time to breathe yet? Feel like your baby's first month flew by—and seemed to take forever? Good. Congratulations are in order. You have survived fatherhood's first test: making it through your initial rookie round. The baby and your partner survived, too.

If you're showing up for the parenting game every day, then you're seeing how quickly the baby develops and masters new skills. You're also probably noticing some developments in yourself.

This chapter takes you through your baby's sixth month, exploring how things roll for the both of you.

Heads Up! Month Two

Babies have fairly weak head and neck muscles at birth, but they get to work strengthening those right away. Your instinctive play with the baby, and his instinctive activity, will build up these muscles. However, you have to help him carry his head during the first few months (see Chapter 8 for a play-by-play on how to pick up and hold him). Cradle the head carefully when carrying your baby around, and avoid sudden jerks and bumps.

Usually, by the end of the second month, an infant will be able to hold his head up for a short time, and will follow objects with his eyes. If he looks like he's cross-eyed, don't worry; he's learning how to use the six tiny muscles in his eye sockets.

As time passes, his large muscle movements become more coordinated and smooth. He may be able to do a miniature push-up, holding up his head and shoulders briefly. When in a sitting position, he can briefly stabilize his bobbing head. He will start speaking in oohs and ahhs, and produce very cute and expressive cooing and gurgling.

He can briefly grab a pacifier or toy in his hand, and will begin to calm himself by sucking on a pacifier or fingers (his or yours). His crying will probably be most intense by about six weeks old, and remain at a fairly high level until he is about three months old. When coping with crying, remember: this too shall pass!

 HEADS UP

Never shake a baby; you could cause permanent brain damage. If you feel angry or frustrated, put the baby down and take a break. He's not trying to piss you off—infants are literally incapable of regulating their behavior or intentionally disobeying you.

You can take the baby outside, but don't put him in direct sunlight, and remember that it isn't safe to use sunscreen until he's over six months old. Don't hold hot liquids while near the baby, and always closely supervise a child or pet around the baby.

His eating schedule may be getting more regular, keeping him fuller, and making it easier for him to sleep longer stretches. Make sure you sleep during those stretches, too, so you can keep up with him!

You in Two

When caring for the baby, make sure you don't get "rescued" too often. Rescuing—by well-meaning people like mom and grandma—can keep you from developing your own methods of comforting and coping the baby. He will benefit greatly from having both your way and your partner's way work. Also, make sure you and your partner are aware of, and talk openly about, gate-keeping during your first year as parents.

Gate-keeping describes a dynamic in many families, in which mom, dad, and others expect mom to direct most (if not all) of baby's routine and care. Dad defers to mom's decisions and no one takes initiative until mom gives her permission. This dynamic is rarely intentional—mom isn't out to one-up you. I believe that gate-keeping results from our unconscious cultural attitudes about the roles of fathers and mothers. However, if you two want what's best for baby, you'll become conscious of gate-keeping and work hard to share the parenting responsibilities and power, taking advantage of your individual strengths. Your baby benefits when she gets lots of time and attention from each of you.

Make use of tools that help you—even if mom can do without them. For example, invest in a reliable flashlight to have by your bed in case the power goes out … or you forget where the light switch is. A friend once got up in the middle of the night to get his crying infant and broke his nose by walking into the nursery door (it was closed). Make sure you can see what you're doing, especially when you're tired.

Relax and enjoy the intimacy of feeding your baby. It is a wonderful way to bond deeply with him. If he spits up large amounts of milk, he's probably gulping it down too quickly. If you're using formula, try using bottles with smaller holes in the nipples. (If your partner is breastfeeding, she may need to express some milk before bringing the baby to the breast.) Take every chance you can to feed, diaper, play with, burp, and put baby down to sleep.

Remember to take care of yourself, so that you can be there for the baby and each other. Follow these tips:

- **Eat healthy, and make sure your partner does, too.** If she's breastfeeding, the baby eats what she eats.
- **Get exercise.** Make sure that your partner has some time to get out of the house for a walk, run, or visit to the gym. Make time for you to do that, too—understanding that you and she may not be able to exercise together.

- **Be on the lookout for the blues.** Respect the fact that you and/or your partner may get a case of postpartum depression anytime during the first year. The blues are normal, but if they linger, talk to your doctor and get help.

Sleeptime Strategies That (Might) Work

The baby is fed, changed, tired, and well loved. So, logically, he should drop right off to sleep. Don't count on it—and don't let me use the term "logically" again in a book about babies!

Getting baby to sleep may be the first intense experience you have with the paradox of parenting. It won't be the last. Here's this month's paradox:

- Babies need a regular routine in order to help them calm down and drop off to sleep.
- The routine that works today may stop working next week.

Illogical doesn't even begin to describe it!

You'll have to work hard to avoid getting too frustrated with this shifting reality. The reason is simple. Frustration and annoyance makes a parent tense. Babies are incredibly skilled at picking up on—and mimicking—our tension. Babies don't go to sleep until they are calm and relaxed, so making them tense prolongs the process.

Here are a few dad-tested techniques that fathers use singly or in combination to quiet an infant:

- Rocking him in a rocking chair or glider
- Holding him face-in against your chest while walking around or swaying gently
- Quietly singing a melodic and repetitive song, like "Twinkle, Twinkle"; "Silent Night"; "My Girl"; "Old MacDonald"; something of your own composition … the choices are endless
- Humming or softly growling, so your chest projects a warm, relaxing, and comforting feeling to the baby

- Laying him face down across your knees, swaying your legs slightly, and rubbing his back
- Rocking him in your arms, with his head in the crook of your elbow
- Keeping the lights on, or turning them off (it depends)
- Gently massaging the top of his head
- Once he's down in the crib, laying your hand on his belly while you quietly talk, sing, or pray
- Anything else you invent that works

Think of these techniques as items in your calming toolbox. Just as with your household toolbox, you don't use every tool every day, and sometimes you use a different tool to solve the same problem (like clearing a clogged sink with an untwisted coat hanger or a pipe wrench, depending on what's causing the clog).

For example, some sleeptime strategies may work well in the morning, and others in the evening. Always be prepared to try something different if (or, rather, when) what you've been doing stops being effective.

During the first month or so, your infant is likely to drop off for a nap while he's eating. Make sure to burp him before laying him down, even if it wakes him up momentarily. An unburped baby soon wakes up with discomfort, and you'll have to put him to sleep all over again.

Above all else, do your fair share (read: at least 50 percent) of putting the baby to sleep. You and your partner will *both* feel exhausted regularly with your new baby. But this is not a competition about who is more tired, more responsible, or most put-upon.

Keeping score—"Nine hours at my job is just as hard and important as changing nine diapers." "No it isn't!" "Yes it is!" "No it's not!"—is (to mix metaphors) a dead-end spiral.

Even more important, times spent calming the baby are among the most powerful bonding moments you ever have with your child. Don't miss the experience because you have to get up in the morning. Your baby and your family need you to suit up as both a wage-earner and an involved, responsible father. In the end, chances are your baby and your family will almost always value the latter more than the former.

Resent-o-Rama

The new parent experience whacks you in the face with the enormity of your new responsibilities. Many days, those duties (starting with responsibility for the baby's life) create significant stress.

You may even have moments when you resent your baby, all the changes he wrought, and his refusal to go to sleep. Most parents feel this way some of the time; it's an understandable response to the stress.

However, your baby isn't able to do anything about your feelings— and an infant cannot decide to make your life miserable. He is responding to his most essential needs with instinct, not free will or intention. Don't blame him for the stress. Acknowledge how much work parenting infants is, and how much your life has changed. Get support to keep your perspective, so you don't let resentment cut you off from the joy that these days also include.

Most important, if you feel like you want to harm the baby, put him down and call someone. Develop (and use) a list of people who will come to give you an emergency break.

This Is Personal: Month Three

When your baby is around 8- to 10-weeks old, she will start to give more personal reactions to you and your partner. She will laugh, blather, and even squeal. Best of all, she will readily recognize your scent, face, and voice.

She can see colors at birth, but best recognizes black, white, and primary colors that contrast sharply. If you put your face close to hers, and slowly move it side to side, she may look straight into your eyes, and follow them back and forth. This is very cool!

By the end of three months, she'll have a chorus of sounds to make. She can laugh, sigh, gurgle, and make other "un-vocalized" noises.

As she starts moving her limbs more, she can start interacting with simple toys and start moving around a bit. Only provide toys that don't plug into electricity and aren't a choking hazard—no small parts that can break off (or be gnawed off) and be swallowed. Soon, she'll enjoy being in a playpen—a good, safe place for her to be. However, keep an eye on her even there.

Your First Talk

As the baby grows, parental duties evolve. Keep being an integral part of the baby's life. She will start responding to your voice, feel, and smell, so be sure that you're around plenty.

Talk to the baby. She's a very willing (and noncritical) listener, so tell her about what happened at work today. The content of your conversation doesn't matter—it's the connection that's important. Try not to use "baby talk" because it's a very hard habit to break. Go ahead and make silly sounds, but use your normal "adult" voice when speaking to her.

> **EXTRA POINT**
>
> Don't compare your baby to other ones, because each infant develops at her own pace. The differences between babies may be nothing more than her energies going into one developmental area; once she masters it, she'll go back to the others.

It is never too early to start reading to your infant. Reading helps her brain be stimulated and lets her hear more of your voice. Developing research indicates that fathers have a huge impact (starting in infancy) on a child's literacy.

Reading is also a great chance to cut loose with your inner performer. Show off your character voices and silly sound effects. I guarantee that she won't make fun of you (yet)!

Bath or Water Fight?

Keeping the baby clean is good for her health and great fun for both of you. Who among us likes to make a mess while getting a job done? Baby bathtime is right up your alley.

The older the baby gets, and the stronger her muscles grow, the more she'll play, splash, and chatter in the tub.

Bathing is another essential parenting task that requires a little logistical planning and a lot of common sense. Here are the basics:

- Turn down your hot water heater to 120°F (49°C) and always check the water temperature before setting your baby in a tub.
- Use toys for baby to grab and play with, but put them into the tub *before* you bring the baby in, so you don't have to leave him in the water to reach for the toys.
- Always hold or support your baby in the water.
- Never leave your baby unattended in the tub. It only takes a few seconds for a baby to drown.
- Wash his scalp and hair every day.
- Clean only the outer part of baby's ears. Do not put cotton swabs or anything else into her ears.

If you and the baby are battling diaper rash, she might not like entering the water, but usually the bath will eventually soothe her.

READING THE SIGNS

Some parents use this simple (if messy) trick to cut down on diaper rash: let the baby sleep without a diaper; just lay her on top of a stack of three or four cloth diapers to absorb whatever she puts out. If you can leave diapers off during some of the time she's awake, that helps, too.

After a bath, make sure you dry her whole body before dressing her again. Your baby will like getting wrapped up in a towel and being snuggled while she dries off.

The baby's clothing should fit comfortably—not too tight or too loose. Don't use clothes that have strings or cords around the neck or that can reach her neck.

Never leave the baby alone while dressing her; you don't want her to roll off the changing table or get tangled in her clothes. Also, when washing her clothes, rinse them thoroughly and use mild soap to reduce the chance of allergic reactions or rashes.

Does He Like Me Best? Month Four

Your baby may say his first "dada" and "mama" around four months old. Some parents feel jealous if their name doesn't come out first, and others claim that "Junior is closer to me than his mom because his first word was dada."

Sorry to disillusion you. Researchers say that your baby doesn't connect his "dada" sound with you or the "mama" with mom until five or six months from now. The important development is how many more of his sounds are becoming vocalized—that is, he's starting to use his vocal chords with more agility.

All of those new sounds are fascinating to the baby, so he will often make a game of it, jabbering on to himself forever. Capture those sounds on a recording device—when he's 10, you can challenge him to explain what he was saying! And when he's 15, you can use the tape to embarrass him in front of his friends—an important fathering perk.

By now, your baby will coo or make other noises when you talk to him, and he will start to put some weight on his legs while you hold him in your lap. His head is getting much steadier now, and he can hold it up and look at you.

He may also be ready to roll over, which means greater vigilance on your part, so he doesn't roll off of something. He can reach for and poke objects, getting more playful.

He should be getting into a regular sleeping pattern by now, putting in five or six hours straight at night, and having a couple of two- or three-hour naps during the day. He may also be able to put himself to sleep.

> **DAD WORDS**
>
> I don't agree with a lot of the ways my father brought me up. I don't agree with a lot of his values, but he did have a lot of integrity, and if he told us not to do something, he didn't do it either.
>
> —Madonna

You Call This Solid Food?

Four or five months is the age when most infant start their first solid foods (which are more mush than solid). If you sample his whirled peas, prepare for a bland experience. Your child's taste buds will take years to develop fully, so flavor matters less to him than to you.

Discuss with the pediatrician when your baby will be ready to eat solid food. He has to be strong enough to hold his head up and coordinate the muscles needed for "chewing" and swallowing (the baby; most pediatricians are masticating on their own by the end of med school).

The baby's digestive system also has to be ready. That's why you should start solid foods gradually, mixing them in with breast milk or formula. Many doctors recommend introducing one kind of food at a time, for a few days each, so you can tell if the baby is allergic to any specific foods.

How do you know he's ready for solid food? Look for these developmental signs:

- He remains hungry even after more frequent nursing or feeding.
- He can hold his head up independently.
- He reaches for utensils and cups, and shows an interest in what you are eating.

- He loses the reflex to thrust food of his mouth with his tongue.
- He can move his tongue back and forth, and up and down.
- He makes chewing motions (sometimes imitating you).

Still Talking Nonsense

By month four, you're probably getting to know the baby's personality and enjoy your interactions with her. You can start having fun making faces at each other, jabbering away, and playing, playing, playing. Keep in mind, though, that babies rely on (and actually enjoy) routine. So, make sure play times happen about the same time every day, and not too close to bedtime. If she's overstimulated, your job is harder when you try to put her down for the night.

When relatives and friends visit, coach them on the baby's routine and what she likes, but let them develop their own relationship with her. Her social development is enhanced when she's used to being held and talked to by others.

If people around you don't seem as excited as they were a month or two ago, don't fret. After all, this baby is having a much bigger impact on you than she is on your officemates. Friends and relatives often share your enthusiasm in the early months, but then the demands of their own lives draw their attention away.

Make sure that your boss still remembers that you have an infant, however. You need her or his support to give as much time as you can to your fathering. Don't hit the boss over the head with reminders, but mention the baby from time to time, so the higher-ups don't forget that you're a dad now (and, you can point out, a better employee!).

Orally Fixated: Month Five

Physical activity continues to pick up in her fifth month, as she starts playing with her hands and feet. As with every other "toy" she has over the next year, she'll put body parts in her mouth. You don't need to super-sanitize every item she touches and gnaws on. A little dirt can build up her resistance to germs, but use common sense.

Most babies are rolling over by the end of the fifth month. For me, this was a reason to whoop and holler, then call the grandparents to tell them how strong their granddaughters were. They loved it. Of course, now that she can roll over, you have to keep a close eye on her—essential as she develops more action capacity.

Your Moving Target

The brain is also developing so that she knows that sounds come from objects and people. With this new ability, she will turn toward the source when she hears something. Just like sight, hearing stimulates her brain development, so talk and sing to her a lot. If she seems to lose interest and start looking elsewhere, she's not acting like Simon Cowell—she's just had enough aural stimulation for the moment.

The same principle applies with the other things you do with the baby. She is responding to stimulation that activates her developing brain and coordination. She's not passing judgment on you, your creativity, your worth, or your love. Sure, she's self-absorbed, but it's nothing personal—because she can't help it. Her "self" (such as it is) has a primary task: figuring out how to grow and get what she needs in this new world of hers. Don't feel insulted by her behavior—enjoy watching the fascinating (and decades-long) process of how she develops the interesting person she is and will be.

In the Swing

The more your baby can do, the more complex your interactions with her become. The two of you become more attuned to, and sensitive to, each other's moods. She seeks your voice and touch, often eager to spend as much or more time with you as she does with your partner.

Be physically active with her. Play with her arms and legs, carry her around, and provide other physical stimulation. However, don't throw the baby up in the air, swing her by her arms, or shake her head—any of these can injure her.

Do not put the baby in a walker. Walkers can be dangerous, especially near stairways. Also, while it may seem counterintuitive, research indicates that babies who use walkers actually learn to walk later than babies who don't use them.

It is okay not to have everything figured out. Your child will never need a perfect father. She will always need an actively engaged father. So, don't fret too much about mistakes you may make or the sensation that you will never entirely grasp how to do this fathering job. Instead, think about how much you are continually learning about fathering, your child, and yourself.

So, That's Why We Named Him: Month Six

As he nears the half-year mark, the baby will begin to recognize his own name. When you say it, he'll turn toward you and maybe "say" something back. (I forgot to mention back in Chapter 7; when he's born, you should give him a name, okay?)

His hearing and speech are getting coordinated enough that he can start to imitate a sound or noise you make. Your noises and words don't have to make any sense; you just need to keep them coming. Nothing has greater positive impact on a baby's brain development than interaction with his parents.

You'll notice more patterns in the baby's vocalizations. That's because his imitations of you are getting more sophisticated, and he's learning how to manipulate his vocal cords to mimic the inflection and rhythm of your speech. This is just one more reason to keep talking and hanging out with your baby.

Rolling over continues apace, and he can now do it in either direction, giving you just a taste of how hard it is going to be to keep track of his movements once he learns to crawl and walk.

Uncovering Your Skill Sets

As you accumulate months of fathering experience, you may reflect on how your father and/or stepfather did their jobs. There's a fair chance that you had your baby at a stage of life similar to when you entered your father's or stepfather's world. Take advantage of the similarities, and ask your father(s) to look back and tell you how they felt, what they were thinking, and what they wished they had known.

Now that the baby is getting older, you'll find that some parts of fathering come easily to you while other things seem incredibly frustrating. This is normal.

Parenting requires a wide range of skills over time, and not every parent has the knack for every skill every day. For example, my wife found the first year with our babies maddening, because she had such a hard time figuring out what they wanted. "If only they would talk to me!" she would say.

On the other hand, I discovered a previously unknown talent for sensing (nonverbally) what the babies needed (most of the time) and then providing it. Their lack of language wasn't much of a barrier. However, when the girls got older, there were many periods (see "preteen girls" in the owner's manual, once you find one) when interactions came more easily to my wife than they did to me.

The point is this: every parent doesn't have to do every thing well. That's the benefit of "tag-teaming" with your partner, each of you running with the things you do best, while encouraging (and learning from) the things your partner does well.

The Least You Need to Know

- You and your baby are developing together.
- Your presence, voice, and interaction are crucial for baby.
- You and mom can limit the effects of gate-keeping.
- You can be a great father without being perfect.

Taking a Walk: Months Seven to Twelve

In This Chapter

- Keeping up with baby's growing independence
- Dealing with changes and emergencies
- Getting help from veteran dads
- Understanding affection

The months leading up to your baby's first birthday bring the first taste of his growing independence. He is getting stronger, growing teeth, eating new foods, and snarfing up more and more information. He will crawl and then walk.

Of course, this places new demands on you, since the baby isn't going to just lie quietly in the crib anymore (if he ever did!).

From now until your child grows up and moves away, your life will center on nurturing, guiding, and adjusting to his independence. This isn't a clear, unswerving journey. There are detours, traffic jams, backsliding, and getting lost.

But there are also stretches where it feels more like you're flying, swept up in excitement, warmth, and pride in your child's growing accomplishments and his special personality.

The biggest miracle and mystery of fathering is experiencing how your child is not his parents. You and your partner exert enormous influence—more than anyone else—on him. Still, he doesn't become a carbon copy of either of you, or an amalgam of you both.

No, from day one, he's an individual. Your job is to love him uncon-
ditionally and help him become the fullest, most giving individual
he can be. You're all together in a thrilling human race, with some
exciting heats over the next six months.

Perpetual Motion: Month Seven

Some patterns remain, but the pace of action quickens now. For
example, baby will still put objects in her mouth, but she's more
able to grab them on her own, whether they're fingers, spoons, or a
carpet tack. So, pay attention to what's within her reach. Her reach
is expanding all the time as she continues to master rolling over and
other movements.

DAD WORDS

It doesn't matter who my father was; it matters who I remember he was.
—Anne Sexton

She can probably sit up on her own without anyone holding her
(another development that expands what she can reach). You'll see
more and more personality develop as she sits there, following you
around with her head and eyes, and babbling away in her own private
language.

By the end of the month, she may begin to "skootch" around (to use
an old family term) on her belly, rapidly moving toward the day she
can crawl on her own.

Your Reentry Orbit

When you come home from work, resist the temptation to show
your baby how cool and exciting you are. You don't have to regain
her affection and admiration every day. Don't cram a day's worth
of father-baby activity into the time between your arrival home and
putting her down for the night.

Your enthusiasm is understandable, especially if you build up
substantial "baby time" anticipation during all those hours at work.

After all, will anything your boss ever says be more exciting than hearing your daughter say a new word?

Make sure you establish some quiet get-acquainted time when you first get home. Eight or ten hours is an eternity to a six-month old, so snuggle your way back into her world, and then move on to the higher energy activity. Remember to ease back off again near bed-time. It's good to stimulate your baby, but allow time for her to wind down, so she's not too wound up to go to sleep.

Jealous or Jolly?

As much as you want to be with the baby, you may also feel jealous or envious of her sometimes. Don't be surprised if your partner sometimes shares those feelings—since we all like being the center of attention when we can. As fathering authority Armin Brott says, a little bit of jealous feelings can go a long way—in the wrong direction.

It's actually a bit childish to envy how much attention your partner (or others) dedicates to the baby, instead of to you. So look for adult solutions. For example, if you feel the need for more time alone with your partner, take the initiative to line up child care and go out for the evening. A "poor me" approach won't get you what you need. As fathers, we are now the grown-ups, and we have to act like it. Be reasonable and flexible, be willing to get along without instant gratification, and take action.

Jealousy is poisonous. Poison is bad for babies—and for any long-term relationship.

It's a Kid! Month Eight

Many parents say that this is the period when their little one starts to seem less like a baby and more like a kid. He'll wave good-bye (or, as you'll call it, "bye-bye!"), crawl after something he sees, use a spoon to move things toward himself, grab things and bang them together, and call you dada. He may call you mama, too, because he still doesn't connect one word with one parent. Consider it a compli-ment either way.

He can pass objects from one hand to the other on purpose, and continues to follow and mimic what you say and sing. From the earliest days, you should read to your baby. That's far, far more useful to him than any TV show will ever be. It helps stimulate the brain, develops a love of reading, and gives you a break from having to think up new things to tell him! (Although, at this age, he'll still sit and listen without complaint to your summary of how the day went at work.)

By the end of the month, he might point at things and pull himself up into a standing position while holding on tight to something close and sturdy, such as a chair or couch.

You Be the Judge

By now, you're probably getting the hang of the basic baby care duties. You should feel proud and good about that! However, other people may not so readily recognize your contribution or how important you are.

As an at-home dad, I shared equal responsibility for raising the kids with my wife. Sometimes people are skeptical that I really did share the childrearing, or think I'm exaggerating because I'm a man, and "men just don't do child care." Even though I make my living as a father advocate and teacher, it's sometimes hard to convince people that being a father is as central to me as being a mother is to my wife. Or, that I am as central to my children as their mother is (the kids say I am).

HEADS UP

Don't get caught up in what other people think or in trying to change their minds. The only important judges of your fathering are your children, your partner, and you.

It doesn't help to get frustrated about other people's prejudices or how thick they can be. It's not like you and I never have "thick skull" moments! Keep your eye on the ball, and focus your energy on how your fathering plays with the audience that really counts: your child.

Staying on Radar

Some child care or health care professionals may treat a dad as invisible or in the way. Things are getting better on this score, but you can work to prevent being treated like a fifth wheel, or address it if a "professional" rolls over you.

"Simple, respectful, and direct communication usually does the trick," Joy Dorscher, MD, says. "Given the many varieties that families take nowadays, it is tough for a professional to make assumptions about who is who unless you speak up. It may seem repetitive to tell numerous people 'Hello, I'm so-and-so, and I am the father here.' But most of the doctors and nurses I work with want to know who you are, and to be able to call you by name."

In fact, the best and most skilled professionals welcome questions and have experience explaining their answers in lay language. So, ask (politely) why someone is doing a procedure, and ask if there is more than one option for you to consider.

"Be an advocate for your baby, but not an obstructionist," Dorscher says. "Speak up, and don't be afraid to ask, 'Can you explain to me what you're after, or why you're doing that right now?' Speaking up helps the professional take you and your opinion seriously."

Don't be timid about what you know from your time with the baby. Susan and Dan had a daughter, and Susan went back to her full-time job after five months. Dan worked part time from home and handled most of the baby care. He recalls:

"At first; our doctor asked Susan all the questions. But I spent way more time with the baby, feeding her, changing her, getting her to sleep, etc. I had as much or more baby interaction and information than Susan, but still the doctor didn't ask me things. In part, it was because Susan and the doctor already knew each other. But I had to start overcoming my own mother-always-knows-best attitude and speak up for myself and the baby: 'Doctor, wait a minute, listen to me.'"

Standing Fine in Month Nine

Your baby's legs get steadier and stronger every day. First, she'll learn to stand while holding on to the furniture. Within a few weeks, she'll be scooting around the room, moving with remarkable foot speed for someone who still has a death grip on the sofa. She'll experiment with bending her knees, and how to go from standing to sitting without too much of a crash landing.

She'll start taking familiar syllables (like baa, gaa, da, and ma) and combine them in varying patterns. So, instead of "da-da," you might hear "baa-da-gaa." Don't try translating this literally; it really is gibberish. Instead, listen for tone and watch for nonverbal expressions to interpret what she's trying to communicate.

Her hands are getting stronger and dexterous. By the end of the month, she may pick things up somewhat crudely, beginning to master that wonderful tool that separates us from most other mammals—the opposable thumb.

Sign Up

Some parents and day care providers begin teaching very simple American Sign Language (ASL) to babies as early as month one. Your baby may understand these signs by six months and start initiating master signs for "more" (very handy!), "milk," "play," "sleep," "hug," "eat," and "cookie" by month ten.

If child care is teaching ASL, make sure you keep up. That may mean asserting yourself to get information about what the baby is learning. Without that info, you'll be impressed by all of her new gestures—but have no idea what she's "talking" about. Sort of defeats the purpose ….

Baby signing proponents say that the practice improves the child's eventual verbal development, although the research isn't conclusive on this. Even so, signing can be very useful in helping you know some essential things your baby wants.

His Teeth Are Killing Me

A baby can get his first tooth anywhere between 3 and 22 months old. Signs of teething show up weeks before the tooth: swollen gums, irritability, runny nose, extra drooling, cheek rash, loose stools, slight fever, or tugging on the ears. Some babies struggle with every single tooth, and some seem relatively unfazed.

Teething is usually a pain for the baby and a pain for you, because he can be in actual pain, and there isn't a ton you can do about it. It can be hard to comfort a teething baby or provide consistent relief.

DAD WORDS

You're not really a dad until your baby pukes all over you, and you clean the baby before you clean yourself.

—Steve

Check with your doctor, but many pediatricians suggest over-the-counter children's pain relievers to reduce the ache and fever. Gnawing on things can ease his discomfort. Try a very clean white sock with crushed ice inside. Dry washcloths also work; they're easy to carry and handy for other purposes. Be patient and comforting. And then be patient some more.

The two bottom front teeth usually come in first, followed by the two top teeth, and then more along the sides. A baby has an average of eight teeth by his first birthday.

If you have concerns about the level or longevity of a teething fever, call the pediatrician. Teething fevers don't produce vomiting or diarrhea; those are signs of an infection that needs the doctor's immediate attention. When baby pulls on his ear, that may indicate an ear infection or just teething pain. Again, check with the pediatrician.

Believe it or not, you should start cleaning your baby's teeth even before he has any. Clean his gums at least twice a day, but ideally after each feeding. Lay him in your lap with his head close to your chest. Rub a clean, damp washcloth or piece of gauze gently and firmly along both gums. Babies love this! When his teeth do come in, use the infant toothbrush and instructions your pediatrician supplies.

Your Baby's EMT

Speaking of things in a baby's mouth, you should know how to stop your infant from choking as well as how to give infant CPR and other first aid.

According to the National Institutes of Health, choking deaths are most common in children under three years old and in senior citizens. The Heimlich maneuver can be done on infants; the best way to learn is through lifesaving training from the local Red Cross chapter. The basic maneuver is to sit down and place the infant stomach down on your lap across your forearm. Then give five thumps on the infant's back with the heel of your hand. See an illustration at the NIH website: nlm.nih.gov/medlineplus/ency/imagepages/18155.htm.

To prevent choking, keep any item small enough to fit in the baby's mouth away from her. The American Academy of Pediatrics also suggests keeping the following foods from children until four years of age: hot dogs; nuts and seeds; chunks of meat or cheese; whole grapes; hard, gooey, or sticky candy; popcorn; chunks of peanut butter or raw vegetables; raisins; and chewing gum.

By the way, don't give the baby honey until she's past 12 months. Honey can't be pasteurized and infants can't handle the bacteria that may be present.

EXTRA POINT

Don't even try to keep the baby from making a mess on and around her high chair. Spread a piece of plastic on the floor to catch the debris if you have to. But don't obsess about table manners yet; learning to manipulate (and toss) her food is developmentally important.

Do not attempt CPR (cardiopulmonary resuscitation) on your baby unless you have been trained to do it. Fortunately, infant CPR takes less than three hours of training through your local chapter of the

Red Cross, American Heart Association, or local hospital. Those training hours are time well spent!

Speed Demon: Month Ten

He's picking things up right and left now—which may give you a sense of whether he's right- or left-handed. The dominant hand will have slightly more flexibility, strength, and motor skills. But a kid who seems right-handed at 10 months may end up a lefty later on. Wait a few more months before you start teaching him to throw a slider.

He is crawling with speed and dexterity now, finding that it's a very efficient and deceptively quick way to get from here to there. You'll soon discover any weakness in your childproofing methods, because he always reaches the least defended area first.

The World's Strongest Two-Letter Word

By the end of the tenth month, he may understand "no"—probably because you're saying it so much as he crawls somewhere or grabs something he's not supposed to. Understanding that the sound "no" equals the concept of "no, don't do that" is a major accomplishment in brain development and consciousness. It's an essential foundation for grasping the whole idea of language: understanding that a particular sound represents a particular idea.

 DAD WORDS

I figured if I could make my father and mother laugh, they'd stop fighting. I stole all their material.

—Jerry Stiller

Still, his brain is still developing. So it may seem like he's "testing" you on the "no" concept right away. If he starts to pick up a dust bunny, and you say, "noooo," he'll look at you. He may say "no" himself and even shake his head—and then put the dust bunny in his mouth anyway.

These behaviors are not disobedient or willful. He is still a baby. Therefore, his "will" is based in instinct and the most primitive human needs like nourishment, sleep, warmth, excreting, touch, and attention.

At this point, you need to reinforce patterns. This has *some* similarities to training a puppy: your responses to his actions need to be clear and consistent in order for him to understand what you're after. Don't tell your partner that I made any puppy comparisons (or name your kid "Spot"); you will save us both a lot of trouble.

Your job is to remain vigilant and—when he's doing something dangerous—continue to say and show "no" in a calm and consistent way. He will catch on.

Valuable Veterans

Veteran fathers have many insights on handling infants and guiding your child as he gets older. Be sure you take advantage of their vast experience. A dads' group is a great way to tap into this father lode of know-how.

You may find fathers' groups affiliated with faith communities, schools, early childhood-family education (ECFE) or HeadStart programs, day care centers, hospitals, or community centers. Some guys are leery that a "men's group" will be weird or too "touchy-feely." However, a good men's group or fathering group is a safe place to talk over real issues in life. Don't let fear get in the way of attending, because you'll get a lot out of the experience.

Besides, if you're not crazy about the group you join, you can find another one—or get some dads and start your own!

Walking Wonders: Month 11

By now she's saying "dada" to you and "mama" to your partner. Even better, she knows the difference. She'll manipulate her inflection to communicate different things. She'll say "daDA?" (raising inflection on the second syllable) to get your attention, and say "DAda" (slight "heavy" stress on the first syllable) when she's pointing you out to someone else.

She's getting more coordinated with her hands and her cognitive understanding. The best example is her ability to play patty-cake—a sort of proto high-five. Her legs are stronger and more coordinated now, too. She can stand up by herself, sit back down, and even squat. She can also take some steps when you hold her upright.

As your baby learns to walk, you can be a huge asset. A number of research studies indicate that fathers are more willing than mothers to let an infant work through their frustrations as they master the intricacies of crawling and walking.

Dads don't abandon our babies, but we're a bit slower to rescue them. We tend to stay by the toddler, encouraging, suggesting, or just being a silent (but visible) presence.

Walking is one of the most difficult things a person ever learns (just ask a physical therapist), and babies seem to have a very high tolerance for the trial and error method. Moms are more likely to hover and worry over the baby hurting herself when she falls (the "error" stage). Dads often feel more comfortable letting the baby try and fail and then try again—which is what she needs while learning to walk.

A dad's tolerance for his child experiencing pain, risk, and experiment has many more applications over the months and years to come. This tolerance is a huge fathering strength now and in the future. For example, researcher Ross Parke reports that "the more fathers were involved in the everyday repetitive aspects of caring for infants (bathing, feeding, dressing, and diapering), the more socially responsible the babies were and the better able they were in handling stressful situations."

Stir and Chill

Keep on playing with your baby, but allow him some reflective time, too. Children need a balance between stimulation and quiet. In his quiet moments, your baby is gathering visual and aural information and doing some basic processing of his rapidly expanding world. He will continue to need quiet, unstructured, and unscheduled time as he grows older.

At the same time, your active, playful exchanges with him are crucial for his intellectual, emotional, and social development. Make sure your play includes a lot of words, face-time, and healthy touch.

If your way of playing with the baby is different from mom's way (or anyone else's way), that is more than okay. It's positively good. Children benefit immensely by interacting with the multiple styles and personalities of the adults who love them. As his dad, you're one of the two greatest influences in his life. There is really no way to list all the ways your positive interaction spurs his growth.

The Least You Need to Know

- Learn how to provide infant CPR and first aid.
- Your comfort with risk and affection are essential for your child's healthy development.
- Veteran dads and other new dads are great resources for you—full of knowledge, wisdom, and support.
- Never stop talking with—and listening to—your child.

Index

A

active labor, 95
Alcoholics Anonymous website, 80
announcing births, 118-119
Apgar tests, 112-113
appointment expectations (OB/GYN visits), 57-58
at-home mom and dads (child care option), 64

B

babies
    birthing experience. *See* birthing experience
    eighth month expectations, 205-207
    eleventh month expectations, 212-213
    fifth month expectations, 199-201
    first aid kits, 125
    first month expectations, 138-140
    fourth month expectations
        first words, 197
        play time, 199
        solid foods, 198-199
    holding styles, 124
    infant care tips
        burping and spitting up, 129-131
        diaper rash, 132-133
        diapering, 131-132
        feeding, 126-129
        first aid kits, 125
        holding styles, 123-124
    ninth month expectations, 208-211
        signing, 208
        teething, 209-210
    quiet time, 213-214
    second month expectations, 189-194
        sleeptime strategies, 192-194
        stress concerns, 194
    seventh month expectations, 204-205
    sex determination decisions, 59
    sixth month expectations, 201
    tenth month expectations
        fathers' groups, 212
        "no" concept, 211-212
    third month expectations, 194-197
        bathing, 196-197
        talking to baby, 195

bath gear, 36-37
bathing, 196-197
benefits of fathering
    children, 9-11
    partners, 12-13
    personal, 11-12
birth plans, 74-75
birthing experience
    announcing births, 118-119
    Apgar tests, 112-113
    breech births, 116-117
    caesarean sections, 114-116
    coaching styles, 72-75
        birth plans, 74-75
        Bradley Method, 73-74
        Lamaze, 73
        Leboyer method, 74
    crowning, 108
    do-it-yourself deliveries,
      117-118
    episiotomies, 109
    hospital admission process,
      94-95
    induced labors, 106
    leaving for hospital, 94
    pain medication options,
      104-106
    participation decisions, 59-61,
      107-108
    positioning self during,
      109-111
    preparation tips
        packing, 87-90
        pre-flight screening, 86-87
    role expectations, 96-97
    sex after childbirth, 148-154
    signs of labor, 90-91
    stages of labor
        stage one, 91-96, 102-103
        stage three, 113
        stage two, 103-107

    support tips, 99-101
    umbilical cord options,
      111-112
bonding, 157-159
bottle feeding, 129
Bradley Method, 73-74
bragger hold, 124
breastfeeding, 126-129
breech births, 116-117
burping babies, 129-131

C

caesarean sections, 114-116
car seats, 42-46
    combo seats, 45-46
    usage guidelines, 44-45
cardiopulmonary resuscitation
  (CPR), 210
care tips
    babies
        bottle feeding, 129
        breastfeeding, 126-129
        burping and spitting up,
          129-131
        diapering tips, 131-133
        first aid kits, 125
        holding styles, 123-124
    partners, 133-135
        limiting visits, 134-135
        postpartum depression, 134
    self-care, 75, 135-137
        avoiding resentment, 77-78
        avoiding unhealthy habits,
          80
        eating healthy, 79-80
        health-care concerns, 78-79
        stress management, 76-77
carriers, 49

changing tables, 31
child care options
    family and friends, 65
    home, 63-64
    nannies, 64
    professionals, 62-63
Child Trends website, 179
childbirth education classes,
    72-74
childproofing
    kitchens, 38-39
    living areas, 39-40
    smoke alarms, 37-38
choking prevention, 210
coaching styles, 72-75
    birth plans, 74-75
    Bradley Method, 73-74
    Lamaze, 73
    Leboyer method, 74
coital alternatives, 145-146
cold weather considerations,
    51-52
combo car seats, 45-46
co-parenting tips, 176-177
CPR (cardiopulmonary
    resuscitation), 210
cradles, 26-27
cribs
    accessories, 29-30
    assembly, 28
    cradles, 26-27
crowning, 108
cuddle hold, 124

D

demerol, 105
depression (postpartum
    depression), 134
designing nurseries, 24-25

diaper rash, 132-133
diapering tips, 32-33, 131-132
discipline
    establishing limits, 167-169
    infant morality, 165-167
doctors
    appointment expectations,
        57-58
    selection process
        OB/GYNs, 53-57
        pediatricians, 61-62
    when to call, 164-165
do-it-yourself deliveries, 117-118
doulas, 54-55

E

eating healthy, 79-80
eighth month expectations,
    205-207
eleventh month expectations,
    212-213
epidural blocks, 105
episiotomies, 109
equally shared parenting (ESP),
    176-177
equipment and gear
    basic supplies, 35-36
    bath gear, 36-37
    car seats, 42-46
    carriers, 49
    childproofing
        kitchens, 38-39
        living areas, 39-40
        smoke alarms, 37-38
    cribs
        accessories, 29-30
        assembly, 28
        changing tables, 31
        cradles, 26-27

diapering options, 32-33
infant seats and high chairs,
34-35
play pens, 48-49
rocking chairs, 33
strollers, 46-48
ESP (equally shared parenting),
176-177

F

false labor, 91
family, child care options, 65
family heritage and fathering,
15-16
fathering, 3-5, 17. *See also*
parenting
avoiding gatekeeping habits,
66-67
benefits
children, 9-11
partners, 12-13
personal, 11-12
discovering your skills, 202
eighth month expectations,
205-207
eleventh month expectations,
212-213
family heritage, 15-16
fifth month expectations,
199-201
first month expectations,
138-140
fourth month expectations
first words, 197
play time, 199
solid food, 198-199
honoring mistakes, 7-8
natural instincts, 18-19

ninth month expectations,
208-211
signing, 208
teething, 209-210
nontraditional dads
co-parenting, 176-177
creating parenting plans,
177-178
ESP (equally shared
parenting), 176-177
gay dads, 178-179
insurance concerns,
184-185
live-away dads, 182-184
middle-age dads, 181-182
tackling touch taboos,
186-188
teen dads, 179181
parental influences, 13-14
quiet time, 213-214
resources, 6-9, 19-20
second month expectations,
189-194
self-care, 190-192
sleeptime strategies,
192-194
stress concerns, 194
seventh month expectations,
204-205
sharing parenting duties, 67
sixth month expectations, 201
statistical data, 9
tenth month expectations
fathers' groups, 212
"no" concept, 211-212
third month expectations,
194-197
bathing, 196-197
talking to baby, 195
unmarried fathers, 16-17

fathers' groups, 212
feeding tips
    bottle feeding, 129
    breastfeeding, 126-129
    burping and spitting up,
        129-131
    solid foods, 198-199
fifth month expectations,
    199-201
first aid kits, 125
first month expectations,
    138-140
first words, 197
football hold, 124
friends, child care options, 65

G

gatekeeping habits, 66-67
gay dads, 178-179
general anesthesia, 105
good touch, 187
groups, fathers' groups, 212

H

health-care concerns, 78-79
health-care professionals
    appointment expectations,
        57-58
    selection process
        midwives, 54
        OB/GYNs, 53-57
high chairs, 34-35
holding styles, 123-124
    bragger, 124
    cuddle, 124
    football, 124

home child care options, 63-64
hormonal issues, sex and
    pregnancy, 142-144
hospital admission process, 94-95
hot weather considerations, 50-51
household duties, sharing, 81-82

I–J–K

induced labors, 106
infant seats, 34-35
insurance concerns, 184-185
interactive play, 170-171

jealousy concerns, 205

kitchens, childproofing, 38-39

L

labor and delivery process
    announcing births, 118-119
    Apgar tests, 112-113
    breech births, 116-117
    caesarean sections, 114-116
    coaching styles, 72-75
        birth plans, 74-75
        Bradley Method, 73-74
        Lamaze, 73
        Leboyer method, 74
    crowning, 108
    do-it-yourself deliveries,
        117-118
    episiotomies, 109
    hospital admission process,
        94-95
    induced labors, 106
    leaving for hospital, 94

pain medication options,
104-106
participation decisions, 59-61,
107-108
positioning self during,
109-111
role expectations, 96-97
signs of labor, 90-91
stages of labor
stage one, 91-96, 102-103
stage three, 113
stage two, 103-107
support tips, 99-101
umbilical cord options,
111-112
Lamaze method, 73
leaving for hospital, 94
Leboyer method, 74
lifestyle changes, 121
adjusting to baby's routines,
122-123
handling frustrations, 137-138
live-away dads, 182-184
living areas, childproofing, 39-40
location of nurseries, 23-24

M

middle-age dads, 181-182
midwives, 54
mistakes, fathering tips, 7-8

N

nannies, 64
Narcotics Anonymous website,
80
National Institute on Alcohol
Abuse and Alcoholism website,
80

"natural" childbirth, 105
natural instincts (fathering),
18-19
ninth month expectations,
208-211
signing, 208
teething, 209-210
"no" concept, 211-212
nontraditional dads (fathering
tips)
co-parenting, 176-177
creating parenting plans,
177-178
ESP (equally shared
parenting), 176-177
gay dads, 178-179
insurance concerns, 184-185
live-away dads, 182-184
middle-age dads, 181-182
tackling touch taboos,
186-188
teen dads, 179-181
nurseries, 21-26
design and layout, 24-25
location, 23-24
planning, 22-23
time considerations, 25-26

O

OB/GYN doctors
appointment expectations,
57-58
selecting, 53-57

P

packing tips (birthing
experience), 87-90
pain medication options (labor
and delivery process), 104-106

parenting. *See also* fathering
  discovering your skills, 202
  eighth month expectations,
    205-207
  eleventh month expectations,
    212-213
  fifth month expectations,
    199-201
  fourth month expectations
    first words, 197
    play time, 199
    solid food, 198-199
  ninth month expectations,
    208-211
    signing, 208
    teething, 209-210
  nontraditional dads
    co-parenting, 176-177
    creating parenting plans,
      177-178
    ESP (equally shared
      parenting), 176-177
    gay dads, 178-179
    insurance concerns,
      184-185
    live-away dads, 182-184
    middle-age dads, 181-182
    tackling touch taboos,
      186-188
    teen dads, 179-181
  quiet time, 213-214
  second month expectations,
    189-194
    self-care, 190-192
    sleeptime strategies,
      192-194
    stress concerns, 194
  seventh month expectations,
    204-205
  sharing duties, 67, 81-82
  sixth month expectations, 201
  tenth month expectations
    fathers' groups, 212
    "no" concept, 211-212
  third month expectations,
    194-197
    bathing, 196-197
    talking to baby, 195
parents
  family heritage and fathering,
    15-16
  influence on fathering style,
    13-14
participation decisions (birthing
  process), 59-61, 107-108
partners
  avoiding gatekeeping habits,
    66-67
  caring for, 133-135
    limiting visits, 134-135
    postpartum depression, 134
  fathering benefits, 12-13
pediatricians, selecting, 61-62
personal benefits, 11-12
phase one labor, 92
phase three labor, 92-96, 102-103
phase two labor, 92-95, 101-102
pheromones, 147-148
placenta delivery, 113
planning nurseries, 22-23
play considerations, 169-173
  interactive play, 170-171
  toys, 171-173
play pens, 48-49
play times, 199
postpartum depression, 134
pregnancy
  learning opportunities, 69-71
  sex and pregnancy
    coital alternatives, 145-146
    hormonal issues, 142-144
    pheromones, 147-148

positioning tips, 146-147
warnings, 144-145
preparations
basic supplies, 35-36
bath gear, 36-37
birthing experience
packing, 87-90
pre-flight screening, 86-87
changing tables, 31
childproofing
kitchens, 38-39
living areas, 39-40
smoke alarms, 37-38
crib selections
accessories, 29-30
assembly, 28
cradles, 26-27
diapering options, 32-33
infant seats and high chairs,
34-35
nurseries, 21-26
rocking chairs, 33
pudendal blocks, 105
pushing stage (labor and delivery
process), 107

Q-R

quiet time, 213-214

resentment, 77-78
resources, 6-9, 19-20
rocking chairs, 33
role expectations (labor and
delivery process), 96-97
routines, 159-164
adaptations, 161-162
development process, 162-164
welcoming other's suggestions,
160-161

S

second month expectations,
189-194
self-care, 190-192
sleeptime strategies, 192-194
stress concerns, 194
selection process
child care options
family and friends, 65
home, 63-64
professionals, 62-63
health care professionals
midwives, 54
OB/GYNs, 53-57
self-care, 75, 135-137
avoiding resentment, 77-78
avoiding unhealthy habits, 80
eating healthy, 79-80
health-care concerns, 78-79
second month expectations,
190-192
stress management, 76-77
seventh month expectations,
204-205
sexual issues
after childbirth, 148-154
sex during pregnancy
coital alternatives, 145-146
hormonal issues, 142-144
pheromones, 147-148
positioning tips, 146-147
warnings, 144-145
sharing duties, 67, 81-82
signing, 208
sixth month expectations, 201
sleeptime strategies, 192-194
smoke alarms, 37-38
solid food, 198-199
spinal blocks, 105

stage one labor, 91-93
  phase one, 92
  phase three, 92-96, 102-103
  phase two, 92-95, 101-102
stage three labor, 113
stage two labor, 103-107
statistical data (fathering), 9-13
stress concerns, 194, 76-77
strollers, 46-48
supplies. *See* equipment and gear
support tips (birthing
  experience), 99-101

T

talking to baby, 195
teen dads, 179-181
teething, 209-210
tenth month expectations
  fathers' groups, 212
  "no" concept, 211-212
third month expectations,
  194-197
  bathing, 196-197
  talking to baby, 195
touch
  identifying good touch, 187
  overcoming taboos, 186-188
toys, play considerations, 171-173
transition stage, 96
travel tips, 41
  car seats, 42-46
    combo seats, 45-46
    usage guidelines, 44-45
  carriers, 49
  play pens, 48-49
  strollers, 46-48
  weather considerations
    cold weather, 51-52
    hot weather, 50-51

U–V

umbilical cord options, 111-112
unhealthy habits, avoiding, 80
unmarried fathers (fathering
  tips), 16-17
usage guidelines, car seats, 44-45

W–X–Y–Z

walking expectations, 212
warnings, sex and pregnancy,
  144-145
weather considerations
  cold weather, 51-52
  hot weather, 50-51
websites
  Alcoholics Anonymous, 80
  Child Trends, 179
  Narcotics Anonymous, 80
  National Institute on Alcohol
    Abuse and Alcoholism, 80

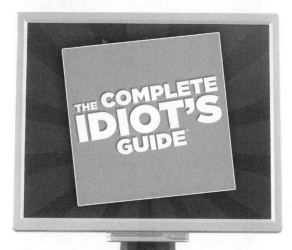

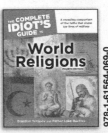

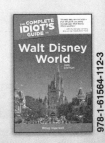